TRUE CRIME CHRONICLES
Volume One

SERIAL KILLERS, OUTLAWS, AND JUSTICE
REAL CRIME STORIES FROM THE 1800s

Commentary by New York Times
Bestselling Author & former Detective

MIKE ROTHMILLER

WildBluePress.com

TRUE CRIME CHRONICLES VOLUME ONE published by:
WILDBLUE PRESS
P.O. Box 102440
Denver, Colorado 80250

Publisher Disclaimer: Any opinions, statements of fact or fiction, descriptions, dialogue, and citations found in this book were provided by the author, and are solely those of the author. The publisher makes no claim as to their veracity or accuracy, and assumes no liability for the content.

Copyright 2020 by Mike Rothmiller

All rights reserved. No part of this book may be reproduced in any form or by any means without the prior written consent of the Publisher, excepting brief quotes used in reviews.
WILDBLUE PRESS is registered at the U.S. Patent and Trademark Offices.

ISBN 978-1-952225-25-3 Trade Paperback

ISBN 978-1-952225-26-0 eBook

Cover design © 2020 WildBlue Press. All rights reserved.

Interior Formatting/Book Cover Design by Elijah Toten www.totencreative.com

TRUE CRIME CHRONICLES

INTRODUCTION

Since humans first walked the earth, crime has been part of our existence. There were no penal codes or written word in the earliest days; however, early human clans certainly had a pecking order and punished individuals for behavior which the clan or family unit deemed offensive. Ancient records indicate breaches of acceptable conduct were punished much in the same manner as today. Minor offenses resulted in fines or mild physical punishment. Serious violations could mean death to the offender.

As a former detective of the Los Angeles Police Department, I witnessed too often the death and destruction caused by criminals of all races, religions, ethnicities, and gender. I saw terrific families, in both the ghetto and upscale neighborhoods, torn apart by the realization that their child or children either engaged in a horrendous crime or were victims of such crimes. Many times, a desperate parent, struggling to find an answer in an attempt to comprehend their child's commission of a serious crime or having fallen as a victim, asked me, "Officer, do you know why he (or she) would do that?" Or, "Officer, do you know why they killed my child?" Sadly, my answer was nearly always the same: "I'm sorry, I don't know, but I intend to try to find out."

While doing research for writing this book, it was abundantly clear that people, throughout time, have and will continue to readily engage in criminal activity and extinguish a human life as unstintingly as crushing a cockroach underfoot. The propensity for violence to occur among some members of society, whether as the suspect or victim, will never change.

This book highlights the finest in crime reporting during the 1800s and early 1900s. You will recognize many of the people and gangs mentioned, such as: Wyatt Earp and The Dalton Gang. However, there are hundreds of hideous criminals that time has forgotten. Do you know of Bigfoot the Renegade, Belle Gunness, or Dr. H.H. Holmes? All were vicious serial killers. Consider the notorious "Baby Farmers" who killed hundreds of babies for profit. We must also not forget the infamous Black Hand, the forerunners of America's Mafia. These criminals were the vilest of society. Many of their lives ended by a bullet or by a hangman's noose.

The original newspaper stories I present here are some of the most accurate and colorful true crime stories of the day. It was a time when society treated criminals as criminals and, in most cases, justice was swift and unforgiving.

Many of the gruesome details in these articles could not, and would not, be printed today for the public to read. Today's concept of political correctness, combined with current law enforcement investigative techniques and overzealous attorneys, won't allow such details of crimes to be released. Some will understandably find the terms used to describe various races and individuals shocking and racist by today's standards. Yet, there was a time when the words and phrases used were considered commonplace and rarely was an eyebrow raised in righteous indignation of the words used.

These reporters were extremely graphic when describing crime scenes and victims' injuries, because that is what sold newspapers. It seems humans have always been morbidly drawn to tragedy. We have all experienced traffic coming to a crawl due to gawkers straining their necks to view the disturbing scene of an auto accident. Indeed, it is so inevitable, we have even developed a term for it: rubber necking. Consider the popularity of true crime magazines, books, and television shows.

Ponder the first commandment of news reporting: If it bleeds, it leads. All forms of media understand people are fascinated by tragic events, whether they occurred by accident or by malicious intentions. This is why these early crime stories are dramatic, graphic, and compelling. The better the story, the more newspapers sold.

As a historian having written over a dozen nonfiction books, I can attest to the fact that archived newspaper stories from long ago are what authors rely upon for accurate documentation, as these were the best sources of information from the era. With radio broadcasts first occurring in 1906 and television introduced in the 1920s and 1930s, newspapers were the fastest and most reliable form of disseminating information about current events. Just as today, some reporters back in the day were better informed and engaged a writing style matching the best of today's mystery writers.

In some cases, these stories shed new light on the dramatic effect the passage of time has on the truth. With the retelling of an event or the life of an individual, accurate history invariably morphs into a version that people know today. As a story is retold over generations, it naturally evolves. With the invention of television and movies, stories of the Old West stereotyped Native Americans as ruthless, uncivilized killers, while glorifying white cowboys and "Indian" fighters. We have all heard stories of the old west lawman Wyatt Earp and his brothers who bravely enforced the law throughout their lives. That is partially true; they also had a darker side, which is revealed in this book.

It is also essential to understand that historians employ "literary license" as needed. When writing a biography of a famous or infamous individual from a century or more ago, not every event of their life was recorded or can be known. In essence, there are always significant gaps and disparities.

As a result, to "connect" the dots in their storytelling, historians will often insert their personal theory about events which may or may not have occurred. The extent of "literary license" employed correlates directly to the number and size of gaps encountered during their research. This tactic is applied to ensure the story they wish to tell is complete.

Adding to the problem of accuracy is the need of historians to draw information from orally transmitted stories from long ago. The question arises as to the accuracy and spin of the storyteller. These are difficult issues to remedy since the subjects and old storytellers are now deceased. In this book, I have not employed "literary license." In some instances, I have combined articles to tell as much of a complete story as possible, and I added my commentary as needed to bring more factual details to the story. In other cases, only a single account was necessary to provide a full retelling.

I have not altered these stories in any fashion, except for the occasional change to punctuation, spelling, or capitalization. Otherwise, the articles are accurate to the original. You will note in some instances there are words such as white house, street, avenue, or river that are not capitalized, whereas today they would be. I did not correct those words. In a few instances, when a word was misspelled, I corrected it; otherwise I left the spelling as it was. I did this sparingly. You will note when I grouped articles mentioning the same individual; there are times when their names are spelled differently. That was not an uncommon error during those times. Often a reporter heard a name and spelled it according to the best of their ability. In some instances, it was the typesetter who erred.

The formatting of the stories also remains untouched. To make such unnecessary changes would be to alter history and do a disservice to these early crime reporters and the records.

This book resurrects astonishing accounts of true crime and will take you on a journey back in time to when these stories mesmerized a nation. Imagine yourself accompanying these reporters, visiting the crime scenes, interviewing witnesses, and composing the stories. These are the reportings of their firsthand experiences.

Unfortunately, newspapers at the time rarely listed a reporter's name. As with long, detailed stories of today, I believe more than one person may have been involved in writing the lengthy articles. I would have included the reporter's names if known.

As I pondered the crimes and punishment of the 1800s, it was abundantly clear to me that human nature has not changed. Money, love, hatred, religious beliefs, jealousy, revenge, and insanity continue to be common motivators for the commission of a crime.

These stories also provide a clear view of the impact of racism on society at the time. Some will find the stories extremely disturbing, whereas others with an understanding of history will recognize the manner in which these stories illustrate the truth. Much has changed, but much remains the same. No law can erase racism in society; it must be erased from the heart of each individual, by that individual. And no one can change or erase history. In commentaries where I used the same racial terms as found in the stories, this was done to provide the reader with a clear view of what the story represents. It was not done as an endorsement of the terms.

Additionally, attesting to the inherent racism of the news media and population at the time, I never found a criminal in any story identified as a "white man." If the ethnicity was not listed, the readers probably assumed the person was white. However, I always saw African American criminals identified as "negroes" and sometimes "niggers." Hispanics were identified as "Mexicans" or "Greasers," Italians as "Italians," and Asians identified as "Chinese" or "Chinamen." No one should be shocked that during the 1800s people of color were labeled in such a fashion. I hope everyone will learn from the past and not repeat it.

Dedicated to Nancy

TABLE OF CONTENTS

SERIAL KILLERS — 15
Belle Gunness
Dr. H.H. Holmes
The Bloody Benders

THE BABY FARMERS — 79
Amelia Dyer
Annie Walters and Amelia Sach

THE HORROR OF LYNCHINGS — 93
Three Brothers Strung Up
Lynching of Negroes
A Short List of Lynchings
Negroes Arraying Themselves Against the Criminals of Their Race
Negroes Lynching Negroes

THE CRIME OF BEING A WITCH — 107
Three Young Women Burned Alive
Ill Usage - Two Senior Citizens Trial by Water

THE OLD WEST — 115
The Earp Family and Doc Holliday
A Fatal Love
Wyatt Earp Routed a Gang of Arizona Outlaws
Shootout at the O.K. Corral
Arizona Acting Governor's Letter Regarding Tombstone Lawlessness
Warren Earp is Killed
The Earps' Epilogue
The Dalton Gang
Bigfoot the Renegade

THE BLACK HAND & THE MAFIA 183
Grim Record of Black Hand Terrifies Chicago
Bad Day for Black Hand
Black Hand Detective Murdered in Italy

THE ASSASSINATION OF JAMES GARFIELD 209
He Still Lives
Guiteau Hung

SHORT CRIME STORIES 253
Dentist Refuses to be Horsewhipped
A Needed Law
Father and Daughter Murdered and Cremated
Two Students Shot
Double Murder and Arson
Two Girls and Man Hanged
Girl Passes Death Sentence on Rapist
Horrible Outrage in Spitalfields
Girl's Lie Causes Boy's Murder
More Than "Jack the Ripper"
Negro Rapist Hid in Safe
The Taking of a Murderer
Wholesale Slaughter of 34 Chinese
Horrible Murder
Two Teenage Female Outlaws
Murder Victim Chopped to Pieces
Head in a Satchel
Horrid Murder Victim Chopped to Pieces
Rawhide Used to Flog Boys
Shot Through the Head by Lover
Editorial—Do Not Make Heroes of Criminals

PHOTOS 281

SERIAL KILLERS

BELLE GUNNESS

AUTHOR'S COMMENTARY

Belle was a heartless and ruthless killer, and the following newspaper accounts are excellent representatives of the dozens written about her murderous exploits. They are gruesome, yet fascinating, and provide you with a glimpse inside her "murder farm."

After reading these stories, you will wonder: Was the headless female body found in the smoldering ruins of her home with three dead children truly Belle Gunness? To this day, no one can conclusively say it was. Or was not.

Some believe she faked her own death in the fire, by killing a woman of approximately the same size and age, beheading the corpse, torching her home, and quietly moving to Los Angeles. This theory is based on events which arose due to the 1931 poisoning of a man by a woman who went by the name of Esther Carlson, who died awaiting trial.

Esther was of similar age and body size as Belle Gunness. What convinced many Esther was indeed Belle was the fact Esther had in her possession photographs of three children who resembled Belle's deceased children.

The repudiation of Belle's body as the headless, burnt corpse found in the remains of her incinerated home, as suggested by Ray Lamphere, her farmhand and accomplice, was hoped to be confirmed in 2008 when DNA from the body found in the burned home was tested. Unfortunately, the samples were too degraded so the testing proved inconclusive. Did Belle escape to Los Angeles or other parts of the world, or was her corpse found in the burnt remains of her home? We will never know. But we do know she was a prolific and sadistic serial killer.

In the various Gunness stories you'll notice names are sometimes spelled differently. This is how they appear in the original articles.

The Weekly Advocate

Saturday, May 30, 1908

INVESTIGATION ADDS TO MYSTERY

New York American.

Laporte, Ind., May 20.

Late developments in the murder farm mystery have strengthened the belief of the people of Laporte that Mrs. Belle Gunness, the most remarkable criminal since medieval times, is alive. With the aid of her accomplice, Ray Lamphere, the woman burned her house, sacrificing the lives of her three children, and fled, in an automobile provided by one of her agents probably in Chicago.

As the investigation into the horrors of "murder farm" has progressed it becomes apparent that Mrs. Gunness was so steeped in crime that she would shrink from nothing. This woman was utterly devoid of moral sense. It is known that she committed sixteen murders, and arson and robbery were to her commonplace.

The bodies of ten of her victims have been recovered from the garden where they were buried in quicklime. Three of these are known. They were in life Jennie Olson, her little adopted daughter; Andrew Helgelin, the suitor from Aberdeen, S.D., and Ole E. Budsberg, of Iola, Wis. She murdered her first and second husbands, Max Sorensen, of Chicago, and Gunness.

She chloroformed the three children for whom she posed as mother, although they were not hers, and burned their bodies in the ruins of her house. She must have killed that other woman whose headless body she left in the flames to give the impression that she herself had perished.

The children bore the names of Myrtle and Lucy Sorensen, eleven and nine years old, and Philip Gunness, five years old. Mrs. Gunness had always posed as the mother of three children. It now appears that they, like little Jennie Olson, whom she killed because the child had become possessed of the secret of her horrible crimes, were adopted.

It is believed that the woman ran a "baby farm" and adopted young children for a consideration. How many of these innocents have been turned over to her and murdered will never be known.

There is one piece of evidence that convinces the authorities that Ray Lamphere was the woman's accomplice. He is a carpenter, a good workman when sober, but lazy and good for nothing when drinking. For years he had been in love with the fat, coarse, masculine creature who enslaved him. He is as unprepossessing as Mrs. Gunness was, but a distinctive feature of his appearance is rough, curly, brown hair.

In the clenched hand of Andrew Helgelin when his body was examined by the surgeons who performed the autopsy was found a lock of coarse, curly, brown hair exactly like Lamphere's.

Helgelin had awakened when the plotting murderers entered his room and struggled for his life. He must have grappled with Lamphere, but under the blows of some weapon in the huge hands and bony, muscular arms of the woman he succumbed.

With this as a key to the mystery, District Attorney Smith, Sheriff Smutzer and the other authorities are trying mightily to get from Lamphere a complete confession. He has told his share in the crimes, or part of them at least, to a clergyman. A part of that confession he has repeated to others. When Lamphere tells all he knows the mystery of "murder farm" will be solved and the number of murders to be traced to Belle Gunness will be known.

This woman's many crimes were so appalling that they transcend the ordinary horror felt by rational human beings at murder, and cause a feeling of wonder. That any human being could make a cold-blooded business of the murder of men, women and children, numbering her victims by the score, seems beyond belief.

But in every particular the Indiana mystery surpasses in horror, in the grotesque extravagance of conception and execution, the Bender and Holmes cases that startled the world.

Belle Gunness was born in Trondhjem, Norway, forty-eight years ago. Her maiden name was Belle Paulsen, and she has still a brother and sister living in Norway. When a girl she was a member of a troup of acrobats, and thus she build up a splendid physique. Lack of exercise in her middle life had caused her to grow fat, gross and unwieldy, but she still possessed the arms and big bony hands of a giant, and was tremendously strong.

She had relatives in the United States, and she came here when she was twenty-four when she married Max Sorensen, her first husband.

Even as a girl she had shown a greed for money, and this passion grew with her. She made her husband take out life insurance, and kept at him until he had several policies, aggregating $8,500. Then he died mysteriously. There is *little doubt now that he was poisoned, but his widow got the $8,500 life insurance. She got fire insurance on two buildings which she occupied and burned down, and in 1892 she went to Laporte as the wife of Gunness.*

They bought the farm which has since become the horror spot of the civilized world. It has been a resort of evil reputation for many years and when Belle Gunness and her husband took possession it was hoped by the neighbors that they would prove desirable residents. But they kept aloof. Mrs. Gunness drove the friendly neighbors from her, and soon the house was shunned.

She adopted little Jennie Olson, more as a slave than as a daughter. The child was made to work from morning until night and was an object of pity in Laporte County. But no one apparently dared to interfere with Belle Gunness, so quick was her temper, so sharp her tongue and so menacing her big, bony hands when she clenched them in a rage

When Gunness was killed Laporte was suspicious. The woman explained that a meat chopper had fallen from the shelf on his head. The coroner made an investigation, but there was no evidence to show that Belle Gunness crushed in his skull with a blow of the meat chopper, and a verdict of accidental death was given.

The woman had made Gunness take out life insurance policies for $3,000 and she collected this sum. After that she began in earnest her career in crime. She scorned marriage as too slow a route to riches. But with marriage and her own possessions as a lure, she realized soon the possibilities that lay in further crime.

Men began to come to Laporte–strangers to the residents– and ask the way to the Gunness farm. They would stay around a day or two, transact some business with the bank, always in favor of the woman, and disappear.

Mrs. Gunness always had some plausible story to account for their going, but the truth was never even suspected until Helen Helgelin came to Laporte on the trial (sic) of his brother early in May.

It was Else Helgelin whose spade uncovered the secret in the gruesome garden of the murder farm. Joe Maxson, a farm hand, had told Helgelin and the Sheriff that Mrs. Gunness made him pile fertilizer on some soft spots in the garden mould. Helgelin and the sheriff quickly swept aside this covering and began to dig. A few strokes of the spade revealed the awful truth.

Not only had Helgelin been murdered, his body dismembered and buried in quicklime, but there within a few feet of it lay the bodies of Jennie Olson, Ole Budsberg and two others. Five other bodies, all as yet unidentified, were exhumed on further search.

Then all Laporte began to tell what it knew about Mrs. Gunness. Many men had gone to the farm, never to return. People had taken babies there and left them, and they had never been heard to cry and had never been seen alive again. It was a veritable house of mystery, because no one in the neighborhood ever went there. When she had farm hands at work around the house, Belle Gunness watched them like a hawk. She had a cellar floor covered with cement, and she sat in the cellar all day long while the workmen were at work. She had a floor laid in her barn, and not once did she take her eyes from the carpenters while they were nailing down the boards.

Only one man – Ray Lamphere – was admitted to the secrets of the house. He lived with the woman for a number of years. Their relations were criminal. Lamphere was a good-for- nothing loafer, and was distrusted and despised by everyone in the community. He hung around the Gunness farm, making frequent trips to town, where he got drunk on the money Belle Gunness gave him. He was insanely jealous of her, and they quarreled furiously over the advances of each new victim. (To be continued in next issue.)

Mrs. Gunness made love to her victims with the ardor and passion of a young woman. Her letters breathe the spirit of coquetry and ardent, imaginative affection. She wrote alluringly of her farm, of her three little children, of herself. She held out every conceivable inducement to men of means to join their lots with hers – to enter upon a partnership based upon equal wealth and mature love and understanding. All the arts of the accomplished courtesan seem to have been hers. And when they came she entertained them lavishly, beguiled them with drivers and with stories of the neighborhood, and wheedled their money out of them and butchered them without the slightest compunction.

Mrs. Gunness was not alone in her crimes. It seems almost certain that she was the clearinghouse for a murder syndicate. It is believed that besides those whom she herself killed, bodies were sent to her from Chicago, in trunks and boxes, to be disposed of. Through one of her agents she learned of her danger when Else Helgelin took up the search for her brother. It was through this agency that she was saved from exposure and arrest.

Doubtless fearing that if caught Mrs. Gunness might confess and implicate them, her agents determined to save her. The plan of burning the house with the children and the body of a woman whom they had killed to give the impression that she had died in the fire was concocted. The body of the woman dummy, a headless corpse, must have been taken to the house on the night of the fire in the automobile in which Belle Gunness afterwards fled.

The intensity of the fire and the rapidity with which it destroyed the building shows the flames must have been fed with some highly inflammable substance. Belle Gunness and her accomplices must have literally saturated the place with kerosene. To make certain that there should be no hitch in their plans the children were chloroformed. This much Lamphere confessed to the clergyman. Then the blaze was set, and while it mounted to the sky, making dawn of the black night, Belle Gunness sped away over the Indiana highroads in the direction of Chicago.

Where is she now? That is a question the whole country is asking, while the police of every city are searching for her. Disguised as a man she is probably in hiding in Chicago or some other big city, possibly even New York, waiting for chance to slip away to Europe. Her accomplices will save her if they can, for her capture would be a menace to them.

There is another question – what became of Belle Gunness' money? She must have accumulated many thousands of dollars during her career of crime. Her farm gave her a livelihood for herself and the three children. All she gained by murder, arson and robbery must have been clear. But she had only a few hundred dollars in the Laporte bank when she died (?).

It is believed that she took with her when she fled in the automobile her treasure chest. She had hoarded the money that was her passion; that made her kill remorselessly, and she took it with her.

Knowing that the end might come at any time, she would not trust to banks, but kept the bulk of her fortune in her home, under her own eyes, secure from any one. Belle Gunness had no fear of burglars or of any man. They were her puppets and she used them and destroyed them.

That Ray Lamphere knew about the fire and either set it himself or aided Belle Gunness and the man she fled with is certain. Many witnesses have been found who tear down his alibi and prove that he was at the Gunness house or in the immediate neighborhood when the fire started. Lamphere has said that he was at a disreputable house some distance away and an inmate of the house corroborated his story, giving the time, but she is not to be believed.

John Moo, a farmer living a quarter of a mile from the Gunness farm, was up early in the morning of the fire and saw the flames lighting up the heavens. He saw Lamphere coming from the direction of the fire. It was then about 4 o'clock in the morning. Lamphere seemed anxious to escape observation and hurried along the railroad track in a roundabout way from the house of mystery. Moo did not get close enough to him to hail him. Another witness is John Ross, a cousin of Lamphere's, who said that Ray appeared at his house at 5:45 o'clock and borrowed a broad axe, walking on to Wheatbrook's farm. Ross lives two miles from the Gunness farm.

Mrs. Gunness made her farm hands dig the graves in which she deposited the bodies of her slain. She told them she wanted pits dug to put old tin cans and other rubbish in. When the holes were dug the farm hands would invariably find them filled the next day. No one ever saw what went into the bottom of these pits until they gave up the bodies of the arch-murderess' victims.

There was in the Gunness house one room in which no one save Belle Gunness was ever allowed to enter. It was a locked room on the second story. For some time Mrs. Gunness had a maid servant, Annie Brogiski. She came after little Jennie Olson disappeared. The woman told her new maid and such of her neighbors as inquired that she had sent Jennie to a school in California. This was thought at the time to be one more evidence of the strange woman's eccentricity and little attention was paid to the child's disappearance.

When Anna Brogiski entered her service Mrs. Gunness warned her never to go into the locked room on the second floor.

ANOTHER GUNNESS VICTIM

LaPorte, Ind., May 27.

Several hogs wallowing in a pond at the edge of a lot on the Gunness farm this morning brought up the bone of a human arm. The finding of the bone has convinced Sheriff Smutzer that other bodies are buried beneath the mud at the bottom of the pond. The entire shore will be gone over with rakes in an effort to bring any bodies the water may secrete to the surface.

The Boston Globe

Monday, January 3, 1910

CROWD AT FUNERAL

Ray Lamphere Convicted of Arson in the Gunness

"Murder Farm" Case Buried at Laporte, Ind.

LAPORTE, Ind., Jan 3.

A large crowd assembled about the Lamphere home Sunday to attend the funeral of Ray Lamphere, who burned the home of Mrs. Belle Gunness near Laporte in April, 1908, and incinerated the owner of the "murder farm" and her children. Lamphere died last week in Michigan City prison, where he was serving a sentence for arson.

Friends of the Lampheres prevented morbidly curious persons from pressing into the house, but country people for miles around drove to the cemetery at Rossberg, where Lamphere was buried.

His confession, made to Rev Dr Schell while he was in jail awaiting trial, has never been made public, although the preacher says that it contains information of interest concerning Mrs. Gunness slaying 10 or more persons for money.

Tribune and Fort Scott Daily Monitor

Thursday, January 13, 1910

GUNNESS MURDER MYSTERIES CLEARED

BY LAMPHERE CONFESSION

DETAILS OF AWFUL CRIMES LAID BARE BEFORE HE DIED

CHOPPED OFF HEADS WITH AXE

Lamphere and Gunness Afterwards

Quarreled Over Spoils and He

Killed the Whole Family

St. Louis, Mo., Jan. 13.

Ray Lamphere, who died recently in the Indiana penitentiary at Michigan City, while serving a term for setting fire to the home of Mrs. Belle Gunness, near Laporte, Ind., did not carry the secrets of the Gunness charnal farm to the tomb with him, according to a copyrighted article, printed in the Post-Dispatch, here today.

When Lamphere believed death was near, he confessed, the story says. Confession was made to Rev. Dr. E. A. Schell, formerly Pastor of the Laporte Methodist Church, now president of Iowa Wesleyan University at Mount Pleasant, Iowa, and held by him inviolate as a secret of the confessional.

The Post-Dispatch says Rev. Schell would verify, if he would consent to break silence, the confession it publishes. The Post-Dispatch, however, says the confession it publishes was made to a man of unassailable character.

Lamphere, according to the story, confessed that he had guilty knowledge of the murder of three men in the Gunness home during the time he lived there, about eight months in 1907, and he assisted Mrs. Gunness in disposing of the bodies of three men.

He said he thought he had not received as much of the profits of the transaction as he considered himself entitled to and he went to the farm house one night with a woman, chloroformed Mrs. Gunness, her three children and Jennie Olson. He and the woman then searched the house, finding between sixty and seventy dollars. The light they used was a candle and they left the house without knowing they had left behind a spark that soon would burst into flames.

Mrs. Gunness' method of killing her victims, Lamphere said, was first to chloroform them as they slept, and then, if the drug did not itself kill, to sever their heads with an axe.

The first man to be killed was from Minnesota. He never awoke from his sleep in the Gunness home. In darkness, Lamphere was ordered by Mrs. Gunness to dump the gunny sack and its contents into a hole that had been made by another farm hand for rubbish. Within a month, another man arrived. He was more crafty than the others, and Mrs. Gunness married him before she asked him to pay off a mortgage on the house. The marriage was performed in St. Joseph, Mich., and a few nights after the couple returned to Laporte there was another burial. Finally Andrew Helgelein came from South Dakota with a check for $2,893.20. Lamphere was sent to Michigan City to remain all night. When he returned to the Gunness home, through a hole in the floor, he heard Helgelien groan in distress and beg Mrs. Gunness to send for a doctor. Mrs. Gunness struck the sufferer with an axe and ended his life.

Mrs. Gunness and Lamphere later quarreled over the money and it was this that led Lamphere to chloroform the woman and her children and fire the house.

Dr. H.H. Holmes and His Murder Castle

AUTHOR'S COMMENTARY

Herman Webster Mudgett was his true name. He preferred to be known as Dr. Henry Howard Holmes. He confessed to twenty-seven murders, but only a few could be proven. Whatever the true number, Holmes was a diabolical and bizarre person. Folklore pegs his murders at two hundred, but that number cannot be verified.

No one doubts Holmes killed. However, he was not just known as a murderer; he was also known as a con man, swindler, and bigamist. As with nearly all legendary characters, his notoriety has grown through the years. Whether he killed a few or two hundred, his story remains one of the most interesting in the annals of crime.

You will find the following stories provide a fascinating profile of a disturbing figure. As with other stories, you'll notice names are sometimes spelled differently and that is how they appear in the original articles.

The St. Joseph Weekly Gazette

Tuesday, August 20, 1895

CASTLE OF MODERN BLUEBEARD

The House Which Holmes, the Swindler, Planned in Chicago

Turns Out to Be a Veritable Factory for Murder

A Sealed Chamber, a Steel Vault, a Crematory

and Quicklime Graves

A Dark Shaft Found to Run from the Sealed Room to the Cellar, and a Trap Door Leads to a Mysterious Hanging Cage Walled in by Masonry

A venerable murder factory has been discovered in the house built at Chicago by H. H. Holmes, who is charged with at least 11 murderers and suspected of many more. In this house built and occupied by Holmes the police have found secret rooms without light or air, a sealed chamber, a hidden trap leading to a hanging secret room, and a steel bound room built into the wall.

The second floor is a labyrinth of mazes, doors and passages.

It contains a death shaft where bodies could be lowered into the cellar and from which a hidden passage led to the sealed chamber.

One witness has already identified the room where Holmes showed him three corpses on this floor of the house.

Another has described a narrow escape from death in one of the dark rooms.

The cellar, where large quantities of human remains have been discovered, contains every provision for destroying bodies. Two large vaults of quicklime, one of them containing some human bones, have been found beneath the floor.

A hidden tank was found which contained a deadly oil and when this was unearthed an explosion followed which nearly cost three of the workmen their lives. Even more

horrible than this was the discovery of a crematory in the cellar where human bodies could be incinerated.

A woman's footprint discovered in the bed of quicklime in the cellar is supposed to be that of Miss Williams, who was last seen in this house, and part of whose jewelry has been identified among the contents of a stove used by Holmes.

Human bones of all kinds have been dug up out of the cellar of this Bluebeard's castle, and the police have found tufts of hair, blood stained linen and pieces of clothing which had been hastily concealed.

These point not only to the commission of wholesale murder, but lead to the belief that many victims will yet be added to the long list of those whom Holmes is charged with killing.

He has already taken rank as the first criminal of the century, but the most astonishing thing about his career is the murder factory he erected in Chicago.

With all of this Holmes, whose real name is Mudgett, and who is imprisoned in Philadelphia, defies the police to convict him of murder, while admitting that he has been guilty of insurance swindling.

Holmes Castle, as it is called, is an immense structure, with hundreds of rooms were victims could be "removed" with more expedition and safety than in the mountain strongholds of any feudal baron and of which none but Holmes has ever known the secret. It was built immediately preceding the World's Fair, and there are many reasons to believe that Holmes, just then entering his murderous career upon a wholesale scale, contemplated gathering in victims among the visitors to Chicago.

There are hundreds of people who went to Chicago to see the fair and were never heard of again. The list of the

"Missing" when the fair closed was a long one, and in the greater number foul play was suspected.

Did these visitors to the fair, strangers in Chicago, find their way to Holmes' castle in answer to delusive advertisements sent out by him, never to return again? Did he erect his castle close to the fair grounds so as to gather in these victims by wholesale, and, after robbing them, did he dispose of the bodies in his quicklime vats, in his mysterious oil tank with its death dealing liquids, or did he burn them in the elaborate retort with which the basement was provided?

These are questions that even the trial of Holmes may not answer and which might even defy the famous namesake, the Sherlock Holmes, of Conan Doyle's creation. Certain it is that as the case progresses, increasing every day and dramatic interest, other victims will be heard of who are last seen in the company of this fiend.

A List of Victims.

The list of his suspected murders thus far made up by those who are following the clues is a long one, and it is alone sufficient to give him easily the first place in the century's category of crime. Here are the men, women and children whom he is now believed to have made away with:

Connor, Julia I., divorced wife of I. I. Connor and bookkeeper for Holmes.

Connor, Pearl, daughter of Mrs. Connor.

Cigrand, Emeline G., daughter of Peter Cigrand, of Anderson Ind., stenographer for Holmes.

Phelps, Robert E., who Holmes says married Miss Cigrand.

Pietzel, Benjamin F., confidential agent and fellow-criminal of Mr. Holmes, killed in Philadelphia.

Pietzel, Alice, daughter of B. F. Pietzel, killed in Toronto.

Pietzel, Nellie, daughter of B. F., Killed in Toronto Pietzel, killed in Toronto.

Pietzel, Howard, son of B. F. Pietzel, supposed to have been killed in Indianapolis or Detroit.

Van Tassel, Emily, daughter of Mrs. M. L. Van Tassel, of No. 641 N. Robey Street, Chicago.

Williams, Nana, of Fort Worth, Texas: was visiting her sister when she disappeared.

Williams, Minnie R., of Fort Worth, Texas, private secretary to Holmes.

Not all of these were murdered in the castle. Two of the Pietzel children met their end in a lone house in Toronto which Holmes had hired after their father had been killed in Philadelphia, as it is now believed by Holmes. This man appears to have been a victim of such a bloodthirsty and murderous disposition that he killed people here, there and everywhere, and often without any apparent motive.

What the Castle is Like.

But his castle, it now seems, as its labyrinths are explored, was his principal place of operation, and there it was that he planned and schemed and where many beautiful women are believed to have met their end. With such a place at his disposal, containing hundreds of rooms, tortuous passages, secret chambers, trap-doors, dumbwaiters, with a rope for lowering down bodies into vats; a tank and a retort for disposing of them, it is hard to understand why he went elsewhere to commit murders.

Holmes himself had planned the building, having no architect, and he took good care that the workmen were changed frequently, so that no one should know what the interior of the structure was like. He had air-tight chambers in a room of steel, lined with asbestos, where the wildest shrieks of the victims would be deadened, and he had a multitude of secret stairways and passages through which he could effect his escape at any time.

The Second Floor.

The building which Holmes erected without paying out a cent for brick, stone, wood or workmanship is a three-story brick, with stone basement and foundation and wooden bay windows. These projections are covered with sheet iron.

The Castle is 162 feet long and 50 feet wide, and from one end to the other is a labyrinth of narrow passages, twisting at all angles. In construction the basement and first floor are peculiar enough, but when the second floor is reached the bewilderment is complete.

On this floor there are six halls. The most peculiar feature of the thirty-five rooms on the floor is the number and location of the doors. There are fifty-one of these doors. They are cut in the walls in every conceivable place.

Their location is such that no room, with the exception of the sealed chamber, is without an exit other than the door by which it might be entered. Some of the rooms have four doors, one opening on each side, and each into a different room. By this means there are a dozen different ways of going from one end of the floor to the other.

The detectives say that it would be an absolute impossibility for a stranger in the building to catch a person familiar with the rooms, either in daylight or at night, for the doors are so numerous that any stranger would be confused in trying to pass the length of the building.

At the south end of the second floor is a space, which is neither hall nor room, through which a person can wander several different ways, on account of the irregular walls. In fact, there seems to be little else but walls in the area. On all sides except one its only exits are through narrow passages, in which two persons could not pass each other. A portion of this space apparently has been used for a kitchen, but the fire which Holmes is supposed to have started in the building two years ago has obliterated all traces of housekeeping.

The Sealed Chamber.

Interest centers, however, around the mysterious small rooms in the middle of the floor. From two rooms which have access to the remainder of the floor you step into a dark closet. There are five doors leading into the closet, making it in reality only a framework for doors.

One of these doors opens into a good sized closet. Another door opens into the sealed chamber. This door was boarded up when search through the building first began, and it took an experienced eye to detect the presence of a doorway. When Detectives Norton and Fitzpatrick, who had charge of the search for the supposed bodies of Minnie and Annie Williams, tore down the lathing and plaster, they found themselves in a dark chamber, with no entrance save the one through which they had gone in.

This secret concealed chamber was one of the largest rooms in the house. It is about twelve feet long and eight feet wide. It could not have been intended for a closet.

There was still no furniture in it. The air was stifling when the detectives entered, and there was no visible means of ventilation at that time. Later, however, in a triangular end of the chamber, resembling a closet, it was found near the ceiling an opening which apparently ended in darkness.

Investigation showed that a shaft ran up a few feet and then, turning at a right angle, opened into the dummy elevator shaft. This shaft is large enough to admit the body of a man, and access to the sealed chamber could be gained easily by getting on top of the dummy elevator at the second floor and raising it a few feet.

The Secret Trap Door.

The north door of the five openings into the closet leads to the bathroom. In this room is a trapdoor in the floor, four feet long and two feet wide. Below it is a narrow stairs, which lead down into darkness.

After crawling down the stairs about eight feet you stand in another secret chamber. This is situated about half way between the first and the second floors.

This secret chamber is of about the size of the bathroom seven feet by five feet, but there is little floor space, on account of the stairs from above and a cut through which a second set of stairs descends.

At the south end of the secret chamber there is a door which is securely fastened. It is known, however, to open on a stairway which leads down to the level of the first floor and communicates with a tin shop in Wallace Street. The tinner has built a bench against the floor. He says he knows that there is a stairway leading up, but he cannot tell where it ends.

The second set of stairs descends only about six feet and ends abruptly in a blind partition of lathing and plaster. The partition is only twelve inches higher than the foot of the stairs, and you can step from the stairs along the plastering for about five feet to an opening into the dummy elevator-shaft.

There is no escape from the second set of stairs except to the cellar. Where the stairs end the east partition is very thin, and through it light sifts in from the prescription room of Holmes' drug store, which is on the first floor and in the northeast corner of the building.

The Dummy Elevator.

The drug store has stairs leading down into the cellar and you can stand on these stairs and look up through the imperfectly built and burned plaster wall to the second stairway. The partition itself seems to be of no use except as a blind for the stairway. The dummy elevator-shaft is about four feet square and formerly extended from below the third floor to the cellar. Lately it has been boarded up.

When Holmes erected this building he said he was going to keep World's Fair "roomers" on the second floor. But most of his guests remained with him only a short time. He had his office on the third floor, in the northeast corner, and in passing from his drug store to his office he always passed through one or more of the rooms.

It was on this second floor that Holmes is supposed to have carried on most of his fine work. The janitor and his wife seldom visited the space and most of the time Holmes had it all to himself. He had electrical devices which warned him as he sat in the drug store when anybody walked over the floors of either the second or third story.

Minnie Williams, whom he is supposed to have murdered, occupied a room just off his office. It is said that she was of a most jealous disposition, and would get it to a fury of passion whenever he was found in the company of other women. To protect himself from her espionage, he connected wires with a certain step on the stairway leading from the third to the second floor, so that he was apprised immediately as soon as she either went down or up the stairs.

The steel-jacketed room was found on the third floor of the castle and next to the office used by Holmes. It is practically a bank vault.

In addition to a steel lining, its sides are covered with asbestos to deaden sound. Its heavy steel doors swing on a big pair of hinges.

Nobody but Holmes could open the safe, which was large enough for people to stand up and walk about inside. The lock on the door was an expensive one, and the whole structure was put into the building at a very heavy expense.

With the door once closed tight anybody inside would suffocate. A gas pipe, however, had also been introduced by Holmes, ostensibly to give light, but in the opinion of the Chicago police to hasten the death of his victims. By blowing in any of the pipes on the outside he could extinguish the light in the locked steel room and the unhappy victim would soon be asphyxiated.

There was nothing in the steel room at the time of its discovery except some old papers, which were taken by the police. It is believed to be the only part of the murder apparatus on the third floor of the house.

On Friday of last week the pick of a workman uncovered a strange device in the castle. In the room on the second floor where Holmes used to sleep a gas pipe runs over the floor. Where the pipe meets the wall it turns down into the floor and beneath the boards is a cut off.

In the Cellar.

The pipe runs directly to the windowless room where it is believed Mrs. Connor was murdered. The cutoff is believed to be one of Holmes' instruments of death. Sitting in his room he could turn on with ease a flow of gas that would fill the dark sleeping apartment and asphyxiate the occupants.

The cellar of the castle is, however, more interesting at present than the upper floors, because it is there the police have discovered remains of human bodies, and the elaborate apparatus constructed by Holmes for making away with them.

It may be said right here that Holmes has all through the ramifications of his criminal career shown such shrewdness and foresight that even at the present moment there are serious doubts whether anyone case of murder can be fastened upon him in a court of law. He covered up his tracks with a devilish ingenuity.

With all the forethought and caution of an educated man, familiar with detective methods and legal proceedings, he seems to have provided beforehand for every contingency that might arise. Thus in the case of the human bones dug up in the cellar of the castle, a game of astonishing shrewdness was unearthed.

When the officers searching in the cellar for evidence of crime had collected a goodly number of bones, it was thought at last that Holmes' fate was sealed. Holmes, however, in his prison at Philadelphia, at once said that while the police officers were trying to fasten upon him every imaginable crime, and examination of this evidence which show that instead of being the bones of human beings, they would be found to be soup bones which he had thrown on a refuse heap in the cellar.

Sure enough and examination of these bones disclosed the fact that some of them were soup bones, which could in no possible way be connected with a murder. At the same time some of the others were discovered to be human bones, and the police at once saw that the soup bones had been purposely so placed by Holmes to confuse possible searchers and break the force of any evidence they might bring against him.

The Deadly Oil Tank.

It was on July 20, when the police were hot in the investigation of the mysteries of the cellar of the castle, that the explosion occurred there which nearly cost some of the workmen their lives. Fire Marshal James Kenyon with two assistants was running a tunnel from the cellar towards the street, when they encountered a wall that gave forth a hollow sound.

As soon as this wall was broken through a horrible smell was encountered, and fumes like those of the charnel house rushed forth. A plumber was sent for and the workmen gathered about while he proceeded to investigate.

The first thing the plumber did was to light a match. Then there was a terrific explosion that shook the building, while flames poured forth into the cellar. The plumber was the only man who escaped uninjured, and an ambulance took the other workmen to the hospital. Then a thorough search of this mysterious chamber was made by the police. They found that the brick wall had concealed a tank curiously constructed. This tank had contained an oil whose fumes, the chemists say, would destroy human life within less than a minute.

A Woman's Footprint.

There were evidences about the cellar of this mysterious and deadly oil having been used, for a naked female footprint was discovered in a secret room in the cellar, and an expert examination showed that the woman who made the print at first stepped in this oil. Was she one of the victims of Holmes, wildly seeking escape from her dreadful surroundings and rushing from place to place in her dying agony, while her murderer calmly waited above, watch in hand, until his deadly apparatus had done its work?

Or was this woman whose footprint was discovered in some loose quicklime in the secret room of this Bluebeard's castle one of his numerous wives assisting in murders, of which she herself was ultimately to become a victim?

These are questions that Holmes alone can answer.

The footprint is supposed by many to have been that of Minnie Williams, the beautiful young girl, who, it is thought, when dead and cold and after the mutilation of her face to destroy identification, was turned over to Chappell, who articulated skeletons for Holmes. This was the woman who was so infatuated with Holmes that he feared her jealous rage, and put electric bells in different parts of the house to inform him of her movements.

What the Oil Tank Disclosed.

Holmes has given no explanation of the deadly oil found in his tank, but the history of the Castle would seem to show that at one time he used the tank for ordinary swindling purposes. A small box was found in the centre of his tank.

When this was opened by Fire Marshal Kenyon an ill-smelling vapor rushed out. All ran except Kenyon, who was overpowered by the stench. He was dragged out and carried upstairs, and for two hours acted like one demented.

It was then discovered that the tank had at one time been connected with the gas main in the street. The swindler organized the "Holmes Chemical Water Gas Company," with an alleged capital of $50,000, and had caught four men for an aggregate of $15,000. Holmes had filled the tank with water, and run a pipe with many jets up through the water, and had then turned on the gas from the main in the street.

Throwing in a handful of chemicals, he then lighted a match, and the gas had burned beautifully before the astonished eyes of his victims, who supposed that it was made from some new combination. The Englewood Gas company finally discovered the leak, and Holmes was arrested for fraud, but was soon released. The connection with the main was then cut off.

A Potent Oil.

This tank, it has been pointed out, if filled with some corrosive acid, would destroy the human body, bones, buttons, clothing, teeth and all in a few hours, so that not the slightest evidence of a murder would remain, and by pulling out the plug the entire liquid would run down into the sewer. The oil found in the tank at the time it was discovered by the Chicago police would eat up human bodies in such a manner.

For hasty obligation of all evidences of a murder no more complete method than this can be found. Holmes was not only a physician who had graduated from Ann Arbor University, but was also a practical chemist running a drug store, who could easily procure such chemicals without exciting suspicion, and he knew to a certainty the operation of certain liquids which would affect these results and which are utterly unknown to the ordinary murderer.

For murder upon a scientific basis, with all of the results of a fine education directed to blocking the cause of justice, no more efficient workshop could be found than that of Holmes in the cellar of his castle, where, in spite of all the efforts of the police, no direct evidence has yet been found connecting him with a crime.

But there is plenty of corroborative evidence. How, for instance, can Holmes explain the presence of the elaborate retort whose discovery was one of the first astonishing results of the search of the cellar by the police? What business has a druggist with the retort, as big as a baker's oven in his cellar?

What explanation can he give of the curious arrangement of this retort, which seems to have been modeled after those furnaces built in every crematorium, where the body is slid in on rollers but a few inches above the fires from the grate?

Holmes it is known never was in any business that required scientific baking or burning upon a wholesale scale. A baker might make some excuse for a furnace of this kind, but a druggist none.

This retort in the cellar of the Castle was built against the wall. There was a grate covered with sheet iron seven-eighths of an inch thick. Underneath this was another grate intended to hold the fire.

A Curious Flue.

The top of the furnace was two feet six inches above the top grate, just leaving room enough for a human body. It will thus be seen that a brisk fire might have been kindled in this curiously constructed furnace, which was obviously neither for heat purposes nor for boiling water.

Then a human body might be placed upon the upper sliding grate and shoved in over the flames when the fire was hottest, to be consumed to ashes within a short time, leaving absolutely no trace. Clothing of all kinds might as easily be burned with the body, and even metals such be melted in such a furnace.

A curious thing about this retort was that there was an iron flue leading from it to a tank. There was no other entrance to this tank. Was this to carry off the nauseous evaporations of consuming dead bodies? A white fluid was discovered in the bottom of the tank which gave forth an overpowering odor.

How many dead bodies of beautiful women, the victims of Holmes' passion and cupidity, have been burned in this retort? How many of the long list of "missing" visitors to the World's fair have gone up in smoke in this fiery furnace in the cellar of the house where they had sought temporary lodging?

The Quicklime Vats.

But equally certain, if less speedy, as a means of concealing crime were the two tanks or vaults of quicklime discovered in the cellar of the Castle. A body put into quicklime is eaten up and consumed in a short time.

Holmes knew this. He knew that this method of destroying bodies is followed by certain states with condemned criminals and that quicklime for such purposes has been in use from the earliest times. A druggist such as Holmes pretended to be would have no difficulty in buying all the quicklime he wanted, and it would naturally be stored in the cellar of his store.

These quicklime vaults discovered in the cellar of the Castle were about the size of a grave, and in one of them some bones were found. How many bodies have these quicklime vaults consumed? How many skulls, how many legs, how many arms have they eaten up and reduced to naught?

One tank found in the cellar of the Castle was 14 x 16 feet in size. It was made of sheet iron and was entirely covered by the cellar floor. It had no apparent entrance. In the bottom of this tank were found some bones, which are believed to be those of human beings.

Blood-Stained Linen.

In an ash heap nearby found pieces of linen that were blood-stained. In another hole in the middle of the cellar more bones were found.

Elsewhere, under a heap of rubbish, the police came upon a letter written by Holmes to a druggist. In this letter, written by Holmes, was the following significant question:

"Do you ever see anything of the ghost of the Williams girls, and do they trouble you much now?"

At one place in the cellar of the castle, buried four feet under the surface, a pile of human bones were found. These have been examined by physicians, who declare that they include, among others, the bones of a child between six and eight years of age. There were seventeen ribs in all, part of a spinal column, a collarbone and hip bone.

It was while digging near this pile of bones that the police unearthed the two vaults of quicklime, and the proximity gave rise to a startling question. In spite of the retort, the deadly oil tank and the two vaults of quicklime, all working at the same time, it is possible, it was asked that Holmes was murdering people so fast that he had to bury some of them?

What the Stove Disclosed.

It is possible, the police have asked, that this man conducted murder upon such a wholesale scale that even the capacities of his well equipped castle were outstripped, and that he hurriedly buried bodies in the cellar intending at some future time to throw them into the quicklime, the retort or the deadly vat?

Even a stove which the police found in the castle seems to have been used by this fiend in furthering his ends. It was in this stove that the police found part of a gold watch chain which has been identified as having belonged to Miss Williams. The jeweler who sold it to her and twice repaired it for her says it is the same chain. Nearby was found a bunch of woman's hair and a woman's shoe.

As to all these Holmes has given no reasonable explanation. He says the cellar contained gas generators, glass melting machines and the like. But those who have examined the retort and the strange tanks say they could never have been used for such a purpose. He does not say how the human bones, partly consumed and unrelated, came into his cellar further than to state that he dealt in human bodies, which he says he got from the cemeteries.

But he has been unable to give the name of a single individual who sold him such remains, nor has he told what cemeteries were robbed, or when. Even if the bodies were stolen from graves, they would not contain pieces of jewelry.

Up to two weeks ago, when the Chicago police began to unravel the mysteries of the Castle, there was probably no man alive save Holmes who knew of the existence of the sealed chamber, of the hidden trap-door in the bath-room and of the secret chambers, with the possible exception of Quinlan, the janitor. Quinlan has denied having any knowledge of the many mysteries of the building, and the Chicago police now believe that, no matter how intimate he may have been with Holmes or how much assistance he may have rendered in some of his crimes, nevertheless Holmes was too shrewd to take any one man completely in to his confidence.

There is hardly a doubt that Pitzel knew of the secret rooms, passages and chambers of the mysterious castle. He assisted Holmes in the erection of the building, and he slept there many times, but possibly he knew too much about it for the safety of Holmes, which may have been one of the reasons for his death in a lone house in Philadelphia.

Canada and Illinois are both trying to secure the extradition of Holmes from Pennsylvania, and the governor of Arkansas has been asked to pardon a prisoner at Little Rock who offers to testify against him. Meanwhile, the collection of evidence against him goes on at the Castle, which is now Chicago's greatest curiosity.

The Buffalo Enquirer

Thursday, May 7, 1896

HANGED!

H.H. Holmes Swings
For the Murder of Pietzel.

AN EASY PENALTY.

End of a Record Which Was Unequaled For its Blackness.

CRIME AS A FINE ART.

Holmes Confessed to 27 Murders, But Some Alleged Victims

Escaped His Hands.

Philadelphia, May 7.

Murderer Herman W. Mudgett, alias H. H. Holmes, was hanged this morning for the killing of Benjamin F. Pitezel. The drop fell at 10:12 o'clock, and 20 minutes later he was pronounced dead by the prison officials, Dr. Sharp and Dr. Butcher.

The execution was in every way devoid of any sensational features. To the last he was self-possessed and cool, even to the extent of giving the word of advice to Assistant-Superintendent Richardson as the latter was arranging the final details. He died as he had lived, unconcerned and thoughtless apparently of the future.

Even with the recollection still vividly before him of the recent confession, in which he admitted to killing of a score of persons of both sexes and in all parts of the country, he refuted everything and almost his last words were a point-blank denial of any crimes committed except the deaths of two women at his hands by malpractice. Of the murder of several members of the Pitezel family he denied all complicity, particularly of the father, for whose death he stated he was suffering the penalty of death. Then with the prayer of the spiritual attendants still sounding in his ears, and a few low-spoken words to those about him, the trap was sprung and beyond a few incidental post-mortem details, the execution, which cumulated one of the worst criminal stories known to criminology was ended.

Holmes's Last Words.

Holmes made a few remarks after he had stepped upon the trap. "Gentlemen," he said. "I have very few words to say; in fact. I would make no statement at this time, except that by not speaking, I would appear to acquiesce in my life my execution. I only want to say that the extent of my wrong-doings in taking human life consisted in the deaths of two women, they having died at my hand as a result of criminal operation. I wish to also state, however, so that there will be no misunderstanding hereafter, I am not guilty of taking the lives of any of the Pitezel family, the three children or father, Benjamin F. Pitezel of whose death I am now convicted, and for which I am today to be hanged. That is all."

As Holmes ceased speaking, he stepped back and, kneeling between Fathers Daley and McPake, joined with them in silent prayer for a brief minute or two. Again standing, he shook the hand of all those about him, and then signified his readiness for the end. Almost immediately afterward the drop fell.

Arthur McDonald, the United States government criminalist, arrived here last night from Washington to attend the execution.

Mr. McDonald has paid several visits to the condemned man since his incarceration, and has made a careful study of the criminal. The criminologist believes that his crime is due more to conditions than heredity. He is of the opinion that Holmes was a victim of circumstances.

A Quiet Execution.

There were comparatively few persons gathered on the outside of the county prison during the early morning and the morbid throng which the prison officials expected would be drawn there because of the execution of H. H. Holmes, was lacking.

The fact that Holmes would be hanged within the prison walls made the sightseers mission fruitless, but the celebrity of the case, it was believed, would attract a large crowd. Access to the prison, prior to the entrance of those permitted to witness the execution was not allowed, and nothing could be learned about Holmes' condition or how he passed the night. The persons holding tickets of admission to the jail began to assemble as early as 8:30 o'clock and at 9 o'clock they passed within the iron gates.

Lawyer Samuel P. Rotan, who defended Holmes, was asked late last night if there was a possibility of Holmes committing suicide.

Mr. Rotan said decidedly, "Not a bit. I am positive he would not kill himself if he had the means to do it. He has declared so to me at least a dozen times, and I believe he means what he says."

One of the reasons given Mr. Rotan by Holmes for not wanting to die by his own hand is the position which such an act would necessarily place the prison authorities. "It would get them into trouble," Mr. Rotan says Holmes declared, "and probably cause them to be charged with a neglect which might result in the loss of their positions."

Holmes' Estate.

Mr. Rotan declined to say whether Holmes intended to make any restitution to Mrs. Pitezel or provision for any of the three women to whom he was married.

Pressed upon this point, the lawyer evaded any reply for a time and finally said he was not in the position to make public what the condemned man had directed him to do in his condition.

If anyone gets anything from Holmes' estate, it will probably be Mrs. Ida J. Belknap, who was the second woman the murderer married. She is living at Willamette, Ill., a suburb of Chicago, and has with her the 6-year-old daughter of whom Holmes is the father. This little girl last week wrote the condemned man a brief letter couched in such childishly pathetic terms that the man who is accused of having killed a dozen people or more burst into tears when he read it.

Although in erecting the gallows only bolts and screws were used, and little or no noise was made, Holmes acute ears made him aware of what was being done soon after the work started yesterday, and the knowledge made him nervous and uneasy, although he tried to conceal it. Only to the Rev. Father Daley, his spiritual advisor, and Mr. Rotan, did he speak of the scaffold, and to them he said but a word or two.

All the arrangements for the burial ceremonies have been entrusted to Mr. Rotan by the murderer. The place of interment has, it is understood, already been selected, but those who are most likely to know where the grave is to be will not divulge the location. Up to a late hour it was said that the undertaker had not been decided upon.

Mrs. Pitezel's Plans.

Mrs. Pitezel has decided to remain in Philadelphia until she is certain either that she can secure some of the money of which Holmes defrauded her, or that all hope of obtaining restitution is lost. There is an obscure chance that the murderer may have made a will, and the wronged woman hopes in the event to obtain at least part of that to which she is entitled. Thomas Fahy, Mrs. Pitezel's lawyer, has little hope that Holmes will make voluntary restitution to his client. He says that in his position it will be necessary for him to attach the murderer's money if he wants any of it.

HOLMES' BLACK RECORD.

Nothing in Recent Times to Match the Crimes

of the Multi-Murderer.

Herman W. Mudgett, better known as H. H. Holmes, was one of the most conspicuous criminals of modern times, and if the "murder confessions" which he has written can only partially be believed, he was without a peer as a bloodthirsty demon. His recent ingenious "confession," wherein he claimed to have killed 27 persons, was disproved, partly at least, by the appearance of several of the so-called victims; but Holmes' object in making the "confession" was realized – the obtaining of a some said to be $7,500, and which amount is said to have been settled upon the criminal's 18-year-old son.

While the "confessions" have served to increase the sensationalism of the case, the only capital crime for which Holmes had to answer was a killing in this city, on September 2, 1894, of Benjamin F. Pitezel, his fellow-conspirator. The murder was committed in the dwelling, No. 1316 Callowhill St. Holmes' conviction of murder in the first degree, the affirmation by the Pennsylvania Supreme Court of the verdict, and the recent refusal of Gov. Hastings to grant a respite are so well known that a narration of these facts is unnecessary.

The Capture of Holmes.

Holmes was captured in Boston, Massachusetts, in the latter part of 1894, by: Owen Hanscom, the Deputy Superintendent of Police, upon the strength of a telegram from Fort Worth, Texas, where he was wanted for horse stealing and for other charges of larceny. At that time the officials of the Fidelity Mutual Life Association of Philadelphia, were hot on Holmes trail for defrauding the concern out of $10,000 in connection with Pitezel's death, the latter being insured for this amount, and as the accused believed horse stealing to be a high crime in Texas, he voluntarily confessed to Deputy Superintendent Hanscom to the insurance fraud. He did not, for a moment, dream that he was suspected of the murder of Pitezel, and he came to Philadelphia without requisition papers. He expressed a willingness to be tried here on the conspiracy charge in preference to that of horse stealing at Fort Worth. Before leaving Boston, Holmes made this "confession" to Mr. Hanscom:

"When I concluded it was time to carry out our scheme to defraud the insurance company, I secured a "stiff" in New York and shipped the trunk to Philadelphia. I turned the check for the trunk over to Pitezel on the Sunday nearest first of September. I instructed him to prepare the body, and

in three hours we were on our way to New York. Ten days after payment of the money I saw Pitezel in Cincinnati. I took the three children to that city, where the father saw them. Pitezel agreed to go South, and he took one child, Howard. I took the two girls to Chicago because I had business there. We all met again in Detroit. Pitezel took the children and went to South America. During all this time Mrs. Pitezel knew her husband was alive, but she did not know he had the children. If she was aware of that she would insist that the crooked business be wound up right away. In order to keep Mrs. Pitezel away from her husband I had to tell her he was here and there, traveling from one city to another."

Confessions Made to Order.

This was the first of a number of alleged admissions that Holmes subsequently made. In fact he acquired the penchant for making "confessions" that surprised the authorities.

The insurance officials had good ground for believing Holmes had murdered Pitezel and the three children, so when the prisoner arrived in Philadelphia he was urged to make another "confession." And he did so without any hesitation, but it varied somewhat from the one he made in Boston. It graphically narrated how the body was substituted for Pitezel in the Callowhill Street house, and its identification by Alice Pitezel as that of her father a week afterward. Holmes also related how the money was received from the insurance company and its subsequent division between Mrs. Pitezel, Jeptha D. Howe, the St. Louis lawyer, and himself. It was in this "confession" that Holmes accused Howe of receiving $2,500 for his share in the transaction.

Howe was indicted for conspiracy, but recently the case against him was dropped.

Soon after Holmes was brought to Philadelphia Detective Geyer visited him in the county prison in relation to the finding of the body at No. 1316 Callowhill Street on September 4, 1894. After an hour's conversation with the wily Holmes the detective emerged from the prison with a "confession" in which the accused said that the body was not that of Pitezel, but was one substituted to defraud the insurance company.

A week later Holmes honored Geyer with another "confession". "Mr. Geyer," he said, "that story I told you about the substituted body is not true. It is the body of Benjamin F. Pitezel, but I did not murder him or his children. On Sunday morning, September 2, I found Pitezel dead in the third story of the Callowhill Street house. I found a note in a bottle, telling me that he was tired of life and had finally decided to commit suicide. He requested me to look after the insurance money and take care of his wife and family. I then fixed up the body and the position it was found. These children you speak of are all right. They are with Minnie Williams in London. I gave Howard to Minnie Williams in Detroit and I sent Alice and Nellie to her from Toronto. They met Miss Williams at Niagara Falls and sailed for Europe from New York."

Between this time and his trial for conspiracy to defraud the insurance company to which he pleaded guilty, Holmes made many other "confessions," but they differed very little from those already given. Each time he pretended to tell the truth, but he sedulously avoided doing so. Nobody believed what Holmes said about Pitezel, and he would not say anything about the children, except that they were all right.

The Truth Comes Out.

In his many interviews with District Attorney Graham, Holmes persisted that the three missing Pitezel children were with Minnie Williams in London. He even persuaded Mr. Graham to have an advertisement in the shape of a cipher puzzle inserted in a New York paper, for the purpose of bringing Minnie Williams and the little Pitezel's back from Europe. The District Attorney placed little faith in what Holmes had told him, but the advertisement was published as a sort of last and hopeless effort.

When the bodies of Nellie and Alice Pitezel were unearthed in Toronto, Holmes denied having killed them. When Howard's charred bones were located in a superannuated stove in Irvington, Ind., Holmes calmly denied any knowledge of the lad's death. When the murders of Minnie Williams and her sister were discovered, Holmes said Minnie killed Nancy in a jealous frenzy, and he buried the body in Lake Michigan. He vigorously denied having put Millie to death so as to secure her property.

The disappearance of Emily Cygrand was traced to Holmes, but the criminal said he knew nothing of the girls fate. The partially consumed bones that were found in the Chicago "castle" are known to be those of some of Holmes victims. About the last time that Holmes was taken to the District Attorney's office to "confess" Mr. Graham lost patience with him. Holmes gave a repetition of his picturesque falsehoods. He actually gave the district attorney a veritable "jolly" about the Pitezel family and Minnie Williams being still alive. The scene that ensued was extremely dramatic. Mr. Graham said:

"Holmes, you are an infernal lying murderer. I will hang you in Philadelphia for the murder of Benjamin Pitezel."

Holmes' nerve was still with him, and he said "I defy you. You have no evidence to prove me guilty."

Mr. Graham looked with disgust and determination at Holmes, and said:

"You will surely hang in Philadelphia for murdering Benjamin Pitezel."

The trial and conviction followed. The District Attorney endeavored to prove during the trial, through Detective Geyer, that Holmes also killed the Pitezel children, but Judge Arnold, before whom the case was tried, declared this to be irrelevant. Geyer had unearthed the murder of the children after a prolonged investigation and the Commonwealth was prepared to prove that Holmes also committed these murders.

Holmes embraced the Catholic faith when it became evident to him that he must hang, and the Rev. Father Dailey ministered to his spiritual wants. Throughout his trial and subsequent imprisonment this arch-criminal maintained a nonchalance that was remarkable.

Also a Bigamist.

Herman Webster Mudgett was born at Gilmanton, N.H., May 16, 1860. On July 4, 1878, he married Clara A. Lovering, at Alton, N. H., and on January 28, 1887, under the name of Harry Howard Holmes, he committed bigamy by marrying Myrta Z. Belknap. A few weeks thereafter Holmes applied in Chicago for a divorce, and the suit was pending until June 4, 1891, when the court dismissed it owing to the nonappearance of the complainant. Holmes continued his bigamist career by marrying Georgianna Yoke, in Denver, Col., on January 17, 1894, he assuming the name of Henry Mansfield Howard on this occasion. A son was born to the first wife and this is the boy who Holmes is said to have made the chief beneficiary of the proceeds of the alleged confession of wholesale murders.

Holmes was indicted for the murder of Pitezel on September 12th last, and he was placed on trial October 28th. A verdict of guilty was rendered on November 2d, and on November 30th he was sentenced to be hanged.

Miss Yoke, with whom Holmes was living at the time of Pitezel's death, was an important witness for the Commonwealth at the trial, and it was largely upon her evidence that the accused was convicted. She told of Holmes' absence from their boarding house on September 2, 1894 (the day of the murder) and of his excited condition when he returned. On that night the couple left Philadelphia and went directly to Indianapolis. The wanderings of Holmes throughout the country then began and they ended with his arrest at Boston.

The Fort Wayne Sentinel

Saturday, March 7, 1914

SECRETS DIE WITH QUINLAN

Man Who Knew Mysteries of "Holmes Castle" at Chicago, a Suicide.

COULDN'T SLEEP, SAY RELATIVES

Once Held as Possible Accomplice in Five or Six Murders.

Chicago, March 7.

Patrick Quinlan, who was said to be one of the few men who might have explained the mysteries of "Holmes Castle," which was famous in the annals of Chicago crime, is dead at his home near Portland, Mich., according to dispatches received here today. Before his death he told physicians, he had taken poison.

Quinlan was a carpenter and was employed by Herman W. Mudgett, better known as Dr. J. J. Holmes, to build the structure which later became known as the "Castle." The police held him for a time as a possible accomplice in the five or six murders for which Holmes was convicted. Quinlan acted as agent for the "castle" until Holmes was hanged.

Trap doors, false partitions and numbers of wires were part of the equipment found in the "castle," in which the police believe many crimes had been committed. Except for a number of bones, not proved to be human, which were found in the furnace there was no evidence that any of Holmes' crimes had been committed there.

"He couldn't sleep" was the reason given by relatives for Quinlan's suicide.

THE BLOODY BENDERS
AUTHOR'S COMMENTARY

The Bender family was perhaps the most intriguing serial-killing family during the late 1800s. On the surface, they appeared as an average family of four, farming a small homestead and inviting travelers to have a meal and spend the night. In short, they were operating an early version of a Bed & Breakfast. Except, at this B & B, many guests never departed. The family systematically murdered them, using hammers to crush the victims' skulls and then a trapdoor to drop them into the basement where the mother of the house waited with a long knife to slice their throats from ear to ear. As with a Broadway play, the killings were well choreographed.

The killers would remove the victims' cash and valuables, and when darkness fell, the bodies were hastily buried in the family garden.

When the Benders believed their murder incorporated B & B was on the verge of discovery, they fled under cover of darkness—taking cash and only a few items of clothing.

Where did they go? During the ensuing decades, various individuals were arrested by authorities who believed they were members of the murderous family. Unfortunately, no one was proven to be a member of the Bloody Benders. To this day, the mystery of the disappearance of the Bloody Benders endures.

Without question, the Benders' legend will always be part of Kansas' bloody history.

Chicago Tribune

Tuesday, May 13, 1873

THE KANSAS BUTCHERY.

Further Particulars of the Labette County Horror.

The Diabolical Crimes of the Bender Gang.

Finding of the Bodies of the Victims.

Letter from a Visitor to the Scene

An Interview with a Detective.

The Benders Formerly from Hyde Park, the Chicago Suburb.

Special Correspondence of the Chicago Tribune.

INDEPENDENCE, Kan., May 10, 1873.

"Supped full of horrors" is a quotation become current enough in these days, when crime, is not more frequent, is, at least, more frequently known in all its brutal, horrid, stupidly self-betraying details; but one feels the utter inadequacy of this and every similar expression as descriptive of the

RECENT TERRIBLE DISCLOSURES

in the adjoining County of Labette. Telegraphic notice has reached you before now of the disappearance, in the middle of last March, of Dr. William M. York, brother of Col. York, of Pomeroy notoriety, and of the facts that caused the words "disappearance" and "murder" to become synonyms, namely: three or four others having disappeared during the past fall and winter, in that region, in an equally mysterious manner. The finding of his body and those of eight others has developed a history of butchery before whose appalling details

ONE IS SIMPLY WORDLESS.

Yesterday I went out to the scene of the murders, – a place distant 17 miles, – and found several hundred persons already there, some of whom had spent the night, and even women – of apparent refinement, for whom that blood-drenched spot seemed to have a morbid fascination. The farm, or "claim," as it is called here, is a beautiful piece of "second bottom" land, undulating gently upward from the house, crouching in a green basin; thus affording an early view of any approaching wayfarer.

This house and claim were owned and occupied by a

GERMAN FAMILY NAMED BENDER,

said who have moved here a year ago from Hyde Park, one of your own beautiful suburbs. A young apple orchard lies at one side of the house, and this orchard, twice plowed this spring, and looking a cheering exponent of human thrift, a smiling prophecy of plenty, hid under its innocent-seeming lap.

EIGHT BLOODY CORPSES.

They were buried in an irregular line from east to west, and each beside an infant tree so pruned as to show the murderers how to avoid digging a second time into a grave. Dr. York's body was found first, and found by his own (younger) brother, – he and the detective, Beers, being engaged in probing the ground with pointed iron rods. When the news reached Independence, a large party visited the place, and soon unearthed four other corpses, in various stages of decomposition, but all bearing marks of

THE SAME FATAL HAMMER

(a shoemaker's tool), or, rather, hammers, for there were two, small and large; and sometimes one, sometimes the other, and in one or two instances both, have been used in crushing the skulls of the victims.

As I arrived there yesterday, they had found in all eight bodies, and were preparing to move the house from its foundations. The house was a tolerable one for the country hereabout, being of frame, and containing in one corner a petty grocery, while across the centre of the one large room was drawn a curtain about breast-height, and near this curtain had always stood the table where the unsuspecting traveler was given a seat with his back to the fatal blind, and in the floor, beside his chair, a small trap-door on hinges. Everything was here just as

THE WRETCHES HAD LEFT IT

in their guilty flight three weeks ago, (they fled immediately after the visit of the Sheriff with Col's. York and Peckham on their search for Dr. York). Here lay the miserable stock of groceries, strewn about and trodden into the filthy floor; here were still the murderers hammers whose disks fitted only too well into the piteous wounds of the putrefying bodies now lying in the yard, covered with rude deal-boxes.

I had heard before how the victims had been stunned by a blow from behind the curtain, and the bodies then dropped through the trap into a pit below, where they were finished by having their neck cut through to the bone, and where they remained until night enabled the slaughterers to hide them more securely, and, as they fondly hoped, permanently; but not until a hundred furious men had wrenched the house from the spot on which it stood, not until the misty light of a sullen day had been thrown

FULL INTO THAT GORY PIT,

revealing the awful deliberateness of preparation, the full purpose and prospect of the future indefinite extension of such crime, did a perfect panorama of that nameless horror unroll itself before me. For many were on the ground yesterday who told me they had passed and repassed along that road, had fed their horses and eaten their lunch at that house, and they agree and all the details of the customs of seating and serving travelers there. A picture rose

LIKE A DREARY NIGHTMARE,

and showed me poor Longcore sitting there with his head against that curtain, which was indeed the curtain of Futurity for him; showed me the stealthy hand uplifted from behind, armed with a hammer, and descending with mortal force on the unsuspecting head; showed me the paralyzed terror of the little daughter in the moment before another murderer (or murderess, for you know there were two women engaged in the work) seized the childish throat and put out fear and life together; then the trap-door lifted up, the bodies dropped in, so that, if another passenger came, or a neighbor called, they could sit and chat without unpleasantness.

If the days were long while such pale corpses lay bleeding under the floor those two women and two men worked and walked upon, one knows not. It is already a dislocation of one's faculties to conceive at all such beings as these, and quite impossible to imagine remorse and a dearth of moral sense that would make remorse and incongruity. But night comes after every day, long or short, and then a hole is dug under the apple-tree, the father stripped of his outer clothing and put in, the poor little girl thrown upon his body (some conjecture, indeed, that

SHE WAS BURIED ALIVE,

since she bears no mark of violence), the grave filled, and the earth raked about and made to look like the circumjacent ground. Some of the graves were very narrow, only allowing the body to lie upon its side, and the first grave was dug like a well, and the corpse thrust in standing, or, rather, squatting.

The bodies, so far as identified, are those of York, McCrowdy, Brown, McKenzie, Longcore and child, Callan, and one not yet recognized.

I need not tell you that the whole country is

COVULSED WITH HORROR AND INDIGNATION,

and burns with a flame of revenge that can only be quenched with blood. The atrociousness of the criminals is magnified by the fact that they paid so lightly and willingly the price of assassination for the prospect of trifling gains; for, beyond the sale of the horses, they realized very little pecuniary, none of the murdered man having much money with them, though two (one of them Dr. York) had expected to carry some hundreds of dollars, and this fact may have become known. What guided them in their choice of victims, no one knows. Many escaped who would have been more profitable prey than any they took, though the former were usually merchants traveling in company with others, or by public conveyances.

THAT CONFEDERATES FROM A DISTANCE

co-operated with them is put beyond a reasonable doubt by the necessity of help in disposing of the horses and vehicles which were the principal wages of their iniquity. Suspicion has fallen on many neighbors; so far without much evidence, except that near neighbors should have known and proclaimed the fact that the Benders had fled, leaving everything behind them, even to the pig in the pen and the calf tied up to starve. The dead calf lay there yesterday, with rope still around its neck, and forming a horrible realistic touch in the sickening picture. One man – another German – was, on account of his contiguity, so strongly suspected of complicity, that

HE WAS HUNG TEMPORARILY,

in order to terrify him into confession; but he confessed nothing, save that a man had been once robbed in his house, and asseverated his innocence of murder, or of misprision. Yesterday, however, when I spoke to him about it, he told me he had only confessed – Topsy-like – because he saw the crowd would not be appeased without some admission of guilt.

THE BENDER FAMILY

left their own team and wagon at the station (Thayer) where they took the cars, and the horses stood there tied for two days before the town authorities took charge of them, the incident causing at the time much conjecture and fear that the owner of the team had been a victim of foul play. Col. Peckham, one of our most able attorneys, is on the track of the fugitives, and there is little doubt as to their speedy discovery and arrest.

THIS PART OF SOUTHERN KANSAS

is remarkable, not only for its fertility, and beauty, and promise, but also as being settled – particularly Montgomery County – by a class of people capable, through their culture and refinement, of adorning much older and more pretentious regions. Independence is, in this respect almost an anomaly, and I have been astonished to find a town so new possessing so few of the traditional characteristics of pioneer places. This will help your readers to understand what kind of feeling is excited by such an unexampled tragedy in an adjoining county.

ARRESTS.

LATER. – A dispatch has come from the Sheriff to go immediately to Parsons to make some arrests. You will know the names of the suspected before this letter reaches you. C.G.M.

LATER STILL. – Sixteen arrests have been made.

An Interview with Detective Beers.

From the St. Louis Times, May 11.

Through special dispatches the readers of the Times have already gained some idea of the atrocious murders recently perpetrated by the Bender family, near Cherryvale, in Southeast Kansas. It is now known that the Bender family fled in this direction. A detective, Mr. Thomas Beers, of Independence, Kan., who has done more than anyone else to ferret out the mystery, arrived yesterday morning, having traced the Benders to St. Louis. A Times reporter called upon Mr. Beers during the day and obtained the inside history and full particulars of the Benders' bloodied career.

For several months different persons have been disappearing very mysteriously on the route between Independence and Osage Mission. Nearly a dozen people had suddenly dropped out of sight in this way, and the matter was exciting a great deal of talk throughout southeast Kansas.

About a month ago, Dr. William A. York, a brother of Sen. York, who exposed the machinations of Pomeroy, disappeared in the same way, and efforts to find him were in vain. Dr. York lived in Fort Scott and had gone out on a collecting tour, riding a valuable roadster. He finally rode down to Independence and visited his father, then he started home, passing along the treacherous route to Osage Mission, and nothing more was ever seen of him.

The York family is one of considerable influence in that part of Kansas, and the affair caused great excitement. The disappearances were recalled to memory and the people began to talk of the existence of a gang of murderers and robbers somewhere between the mission and Independence.

On the route between these places is a dismal stretch of prairie, sparsely settled. Two of the landmarks of this prairie are Drum Creek and Big Hill. Midway between them lived the Bender family, consisting of the old man and the old woman, a young man who passed as a son of Bender, and a young woman who passed as the daughter of the old woman. The young people passed as married, although the younger Mrs. Bender bore a very slippery character on the point of morality.

Bender had a frame house of several rooms, which he had built upon a claim. He professed to keep a grocery in the front room of the house, and an eating-room for travelers. The place was considered a kind of halfway stopping place. The house stood in the midst of a prairie, with nothing to break the view for a mile around.

The younger Mrs. Bender professed to be a spiritual medium, and held occasional séances. She also had a card in one or two of the country papers, inviting calls from those who desire to have the future revealed.

About two weeks ago or more, Senator York organize the party and scoured the country far and wide to find some trace of his brother. In the course of their ride they halted at the Bender place to feed. Young Bender, when he heard of their mission, volunteered his services to aid in the search.

The visit occurred on Wednesday. The younger woman also called Senator York aside and, telling of her powers, proposed to hold a séance on the next Friday night, saying that if he would come she would reveal the whereabouts of his brother. York paid little or no attention to this, and the party soon passed on.

About two weeks ago, Mr. Thomas Beers, who has been a Kansas detective for ten years or more, was urgently requested by Senator York to take hold of the case, and he did so.

Day and night he traveled the route between Osage Mission and Independence, seeking to solve the mystery. He soon struck the trail of a desperado with whom he was acquainted. The man had served several times in the Penitentiary, and there was nothing to show that he had reformed. Beers found that this man was traveling back and forth between the Mission and Independence, and he shadowed him closely. Wherever the man stopped Beers waited and learned his conversation. He found that the villain was talking freely about the mysterious disappearances.

At one place he told a woman about the murder of a little girl 7 or 8 years old, and when the horrified listener exclaimed, "How could they do it?" he exclaimed, "Why, they strangled her." This was told to Beers, and he knew he had a clue.

At another place the disappearance of York was the topic, and the man confidentially said they would never find York, for he had been burned in a cornfield and the ground had been ploughed over.

Beers heard this, too, and some other things. Then he learned that the Benders had suddenly disappeared, and he began to see light. He went back to Independence, told York his suspicions, asked him to go with him in order to identify anything that might be found, which had belonged to his brother. York put but little confidence in the detective's suspicions, and sent a younger brother with him.

Beers went from Independence to Cherryvale by rail, and then taking a wagon rode out to the Bender claim, a few miles off. The place had been deserted hastily, but there were plain evidences that great efforts have been made to burn clothing, pieces of harness, and papers. There was a small stock of groceries in the front room. Between this and the next room only the joists had been put up, and a sheet was hung up on these for a screen.

The Benders had gone, apparently taking nothing but a little wearing apparel with them. As they searched the house, Beers told young York to keep a sharp lookout for anything which might have been his brothers. He did so, before they had gone far he picked up a piece of his brothers bridle.

Then the search began in earnest. In groping about in the room back of the grocery, Beers found a little trap-door and raised it. There came up a sickening stench, peculiar to decomposing human remains. Almost nauseated, Beers and his little posse examined the place. The trap opened into a pit about six feet deep, and this had a passage opening out under the foundations. They made a careful examination of the pit, and found the soil saturated with what was plainly human gore. Back of the house was a piece of ground, perhaps an acre and a half in extent, which had been broken up and apparently recently plowed.

Beers subsequently learned that Bender had ploughed this ground over the day after Senator York and his friends had been there on their search.

The detective at once began the examination of this ground, and, taking young York with him, started diagonally for the southwest corner, intending to begin a systematic search, looking carefully for any appearance of subsoil or disturbance.

A few rods from the corner Beers stopped and looked about him. Young York, who is on his right, a few feet from him, turned and came toward him. Glancing down, Beers saw between them a little depression, and some appearance of subsoil. Both noticed it, and the detective said: "There's something here. York; go get a wagon rod." York complied, and soon returned.

Beers took the rod and gradually pushed it down until it struck hard ground just as it reached the ring. Then drawing it out he found that he had plunged the iron into what appeared to be human remains.

The others, who had in the meantime been rummaging the house, were summoned, and digging was commenced. About four feet below the surface they came upon a body partially decomposed, and lying face downwards. Then they stopped the disinterring and began to dig down a trench two feet wide on one side of the grave, toward which the face was turned a little.

While they were thus employed a party arrived from Cherryvale having gained an inkling of what was going on. Among the newcomers was a doctor who had been sent out by Senator York.

The trench was lowered below the level of the bottom of the grave and the earth dug away carefully from the face and head of the body. Then the detective, seeing that from the condition of the corpse the utmost care would be necessary in order to ensure recognition, told the doctor he must detach the head from the trunk. It was done, and having been carefully cleaned, was lifted out and placed on a sheet brought from the house. The countenance was exposed to view and in an instant the features of Dr. York were recognized.

Some of the men there sat down and cried like children, others turned away sickened, while with others the site only nerved them to continue the search.

While the detective was telling this heart-sickening story to the Times reporter, he would stop as he came to this horrible scene, at the finding of Dr. York's body, and seem to forget the present and go back, and his agitation, to that terrible morning of the 5th of May.

The work went on and other bodies were found, until, and all, nine had been unearthed when Beers left. In every case, except that of the little girl, the skull was broken in the back of the head.

The detective is of the opinion that the murders were done in the following manner:

The parties either came or were enticed to the house where the young woman engaged them in conversation, for she had the reputation in all that part of the county of being a good talker. Then one of the men would strike the visitor on the back of the head, felling him to the floor, when the other would strike him with a heavier sludge-like instrument. Then it would be but the work of an instant to drag the victim to the trap and cut his throat. In every case, except that of the child, these terrible wounds were found in the back of the head, and the throats were gashed from ear to ear. Two hammers were found in the house, which had evidently been used in the manner described.

There was also something very peculiar about the manner of burial. The graves are all from three to five feet deep. The bodies were straightened out with the right hand-drawn up and laid flat upon the right breast. The left arm and hand were stretched straight beside the body. This Mr. Beers informed the reporter has been a past signed between a large gang of cut-throats and horse-thieves working along the route from the mission to Independence.

The news of the finding of York's body spread like wildfire, and before night scores of men had flocked to the place to aid in the search. Among them came a German, wholly innocent of wrong, but because he happened to be of the same nationality as the Benders, the crowd strung him up three times to make him confess, and finally desisted upon Beers' declaration that the man was innocent.

About a year ago there was another member of the Bender family, a young man, but he all at once disappeared. The supposition is that, in attempting to dispose of some victim, he was either killed or mortally wounded, and then secretly buried.

Of the bodies found thus far, nearly all have been missed since last October. H. Longchor, one of the victims, was a farmer in Howard County. He sold out his claim, and, taking his little girl 8 years old, he started for Iowa with his team. The last known of him was when he camped on Drum Creek. He could be traced no farther, and the finding of his body in Benders field with the remains of the child a little way off, solved the mystery. A day or two after Longchor was lost, his team was found about sixteen miles south of the Bender place. It had evidently been driven there in great haste and abandoned. At several points on the line between the Bender place in the spot where the team was found, several persons were told of seeing the team go past at a furious rate, and on this line were found, at intervals, the endboard of Longchor's wagon and his guns, which had fallen out in the hasty drive.

The Benders talked boldly about this disappearance, and insinuated that the man must have been shot down on Drum Creek.

W. F. McCarthy, another of the victims, was a Howard County farmer. He was formally in the one Hundred and Twenty-third Illinois infantry. He had had a long dispute about his claim with a man who belonged to the Bender gang. The latter had taken him away to have a settlement, and he was never seen afterward to his body was unearthed. The supposition is that he was enticed to Benders, and murdered in the same manner as the others.

B. F. McKenzie was a farmer from Ohio, who was looking about for lands. He had $6,000 or $7,000 and disappeared as mysteriously as the others. His body was found also.

Another man named Boyle, who started from Independence to Mission with $700 in his possession was found also.

Two others were identified, but the rest of the bodies were not recognizable.

Nearly all of the victims had teams or saddle horses. In two instances the wagons were found on the prairie, and in one instance a horse which had been peculiarly marked was left with the wagon.

In the other cases the horses were run off by some members of the gang, and disappeared as mysteriously as their owners. Dr. York, when he disappeared, had with him a very fleet and valuable roadster.

It seems that after the visit of Senator York and his party, the Benders took the alarm. The next morning the old man plowed the field, and shortly afterwards they hitched up and drove to Thayer, a station on the Gulf road, 20 or 25 miles away where they were not known, arriving there in time to take a night train. It seems that they stopped a little way out of town, unharnessed the horses, and tied them to the wagon. Then leaving the dog with the team, they went to the depot and left.

The team remained out of town two or three days, no one knowing to whom it belonged. Finally, the Town Marshal went out and brought it in.

A day or two after that some country people were in town, and one of them noticing the dog which had been left with the team, exclaimed: "Why, there's old Benders dog!"

This led to some explanations, and the team was readily identified. This led to a visit to the Bender place, and then it was discovered that the whole family had departed. This was just before or about the time that the detective made his visit to the claim.

As soon as the bodies were unearthed, Beers entered upon his search for the criminals. He found that the Benders were co-operating with a band of thieves, and just before he left Kansas, had sworn out warrants for the arrests of twenty-two parties, many of them professedly farmers, holding claims in Southern Kansas.

Beers himself has assumed the difficult task of hunting down the four members of the Bender family. He succeeded in tracing them until they left the state, and then had an interview with the governor of Kansas, who authorized him to go ahead and hunt down the murderers regardless of expense.

With this understanding he started and arrived in St. Louis yesterday, having followed a clear trail to this place.

The Benders left Kansas with about $10,000, and Beers thinks that they have gone straight to the seaboard with the intention of hiding across the ocean.

He will follow as fast as the trail can be picked up. Chief McDonough will render every assistance possible. Information has been received already of parties here who have told more about the murders than they ought to know as innocent people.

Detective Beers says the people of Southern Kansas are terribly excited over the discoveries, and it would be a difficult task to keep the Benders out of the hands of a mob if they should be taken back now.

The claim upon which the bodies were found, he says, is being visited by hundreds and thousands, who come from many miles. The lot was carefully and deeply plowed over before all the bodies were found, and it is not known yet but that there may be other victims buried near the bloody home of the Benders.

Beers is almost worn out with the terrible strain he has been under for two weeks, and when visited yesterday by the Times reporter, was trying to recuperate a little. He will set to work this morning in full earnest.

THE BABY FARMERS

AUTHOR'S COMMENTARY

During the Victorian era, "Baby Farming" was primarily practiced in England and, to a lesser degree, in America and Australia. It was a simple concept: poor people and people who, for a variety of reasons, did not want or could not care for their infant would "sell" their child to a "Baby Farmer." In other situations, for payment, the farmer would care for the child for a specified time. Occasionally, this included breastfeeding and adoption of the infant by the "Farmer" or another individual arranged by the "Farmer." For the poor, it was a method to obtain some compensation and the belief their child would be raised in a proper and caring environment where the child's needs would be met.

Unfortunately, there were several female "farmers" in England who took in an infant for a sum of money and shortly afterward killed the child. It was a horrendous practice. The number of infants who were murdered due to this practice is unknown, however conservative figures place the number of infants killed by "farmers" into the thousands.

The following stories from England represent just a few of the most notorious "farmers." The term "gaol" means jail. The terms pound and stone are denominations of British currency.

Little Falls Weekly Transcript

Friday, June 19, 1896

HUNDREDS OF VICTIMS

Amelia Dyer,
Baby Farmer and Strangler

Not since the terrible murders in Whitechapel has London been so shocked and interested as it has been during the last few weeks by the wholesale murder of the infant children of which Amelia Dyer is now awaiting trial.

A coroner's jury found the woman guilty of willful murder some days ago. There is overwhelming evidence connecting her with the murder of several children, who were strangled and thrown into the Thames, after weights have been attached to their bodies, and the woman has practically confessed her guilt.

If the police are justified in assuming – as they do – that many of the children whose bodies have been taken from the river, or who are still mysteriously missing, met death at the hands of the notorious baby farmer or her accomplices, the woman is a murderess hundreds of times over and stands in the front rank of the unique criminals of the age.

The woman murdered for gain primarily, but there is in the history of her crimes a suggestion that she was in love with the appalling work which made her rich, and so found double pleasure in the wholesale disposal of her victims.

While no correct assessment of the number of babies she killed can yet be made, because the inhuman parents who bargained with the baby farmer are naturally anxious to conceal their guilt, the police believe that her victims will be numbered by hundreds.

The police have succeeded in securing the evidence of several mothers, among them being Evelina Edith Marnon.

When arrested, Mrs. Dyer was living at 45 Kingston road, Reading. Reading is a borough about 38 miles to the southwest of London, situated on the Kennet River, near its junction with the Thames. Mrs. Dyer was generally reputed to be very pious. Over the door of her home was a figure of Christ, beneath which was the inscription, "Suffer little children to come unto me, and forbid them not, for of such is the kingdom of heaven."

Alas! The children who were suffered to come to this terrible old ogre found their way only too soon to the kingdom of heaven.

It has been proved that since Christmas 20 children were entrusted to Mrs. Dyer's keeping that only 4 are living. The others have vanished. Prior to Christmas many of the children who had been placed in her charge disappeared.

Mrs. Dyer was first charged with the murder of an unknown female child, 16 months old, whose body was found floating in the Thames. The date of this murder was believed to be about March 20.

An autopsy proved that the death was due to strangulation, and on a piece of paper found in the parcel in which the child was wrapped was discovered an address which led the police to Mrs. Dyer's place in Caversham. From there she was traced to Kensington Road.

As soon as Mrs. Dyer was safe in custody the Thames, near Caversham weir, close by Reading, was dragged. Another body was found, with a piece of tape tied about the neck, and a little later a bag containing the bodies of two infants and some bricks was fished up. In the River Kennet, at Reading, still another body was recovered. In every case an autopsy proved that the infant had been strangled before it was thrown into the water.

Evelina Edith Marnon, a single woman, who lived in Cheltenham, testified that she answered an advertisement relating to the adoption of a baby, which she saw in a Bristol newspaper in February. The advertisement was signed "Mrs. Scott," whose address was 45 Kensington road., Oxford road, Reading. She received the following reply under date of March 20:

> Dear Madam – in reference to your letter as to the adoption of a child, I write to say should be glad to have a dear little baby girl, one I could bring up and call my own. First I must tell you that we are plain, honest, homely people, in fairly good circumstances. We live in our own house and have a good and comfortable home. We are out in the country and sometimes I am alone a great deal.
>
> I don't want a child for money's sake, but for company and as a home comfort. I have no children of my own, and a child with me will have a good home and the mother's care. We belong to the Church of England, and, although I want to bring the child up as my own, I would not mind the mother coming to see it at any time.
>
> It is always a satisfaction to a mother to know that her child is going on all right. I only hope that we come to terms. I should be glad to have the baby as soon as possible.
>
> If I could come for her at once, I would not mind paying my fare one way. I should break my journey to Cheltenham at Gloucester, where I have a friend. Kindly let me have an early reply. I can give you good references and any questions you may care to ask I shall be glad to answer.
>
> I am, yours respectfully, A. Harding.

She wrote in turn, asking for full particulars and saying that if she parted with her child she certainly would wish to visit it. She asked also about terms, and on March 25 she received the following:

> My Dear Madam– your letter just to hand, and I shall only be too pleased for yourself or any friends to come and see baby and us. We don't have many visitors out here in the country. I should really like you to know that the pretty child was with some one who would really care for her, and you would feel more comfortable I know. I promise you faithfully that if you will send her to me I will do mother's duty for her and bring her up as my own. When you come afterward, you will see I have done my duty. Dear child: I shall only be too glad to have been an and I will take her entirely for 10 pounds. She shall be no further expense to you.
>
> I am yours ever faithfully, A. Harding.

True to her promise, Mrs. Dyer "took her entirely." That meant that the single woman was not to be troubled in after life by specters of the past. Mrs. Harding, or Dyer, called on March 31 for the baby.

She signed an agreement by which, for $50, she was to take care of the child and rear it as her own. The agreement ran as follows:

> I, Annie Harding of 45 Kensington Rd., Oxford road, Reading, in consideration of the sum of 10 pounds, paid to me by Evelina Edith Marnon, when, do hereby agree to adopt Doris, the child of the said Evelina Edith Marnon, and to bring up the said child as my own without any further compensation over and above the aforementioned sum of 10 pounds.

As witness hereunto we have this day, the 31st day of March, in the year of our Lord 1896, subscribed our names.

Annie Harding

Evelina Edith Marnon.

In the presence of Martha Dostnett, widow, of No. 23 Manchester street, in Cheltenham.

Mrs. Harding took Doris with her that afternoon, and Miss Marnon accompanied her on the train as far as to Gloucester. At Gloucester Mrs. Harding bade her goodbye and took the train for Reading. Mrs. Marnon received this letter on April 2:

> When I got home last night, a wire was waiting for me saying my sister was dangerously ill, so I came this morning. My dear little girl is a traveler, and no mistake. She did not mind the journey. Slept all the way. I shall stop now till Saturday. Shall write again Sunday. Shall write a longer one next time.
>
> Yours with love, A. Harding.

In a few days the mother wrote to Mrs. Dyer's address, asking for news of the baby. She received no reply. On April 11 she was led to the district mortuary, where lay the bodies fished out of the Thames. One of the dead children was hers. There was a mark about the neck where tape had been knotted by the person who strangled it. The bag in which the bodies were found the witness identified as one which Mrs. Dyer, or Harding, had carried on the day she called for the child.

The police discovered in pawnshops and in Mrs. Dyer's house more than 300 pounds of baby clothes, which had been stripped from her victims.

Miss Marnon's experience was like that of many other mothers. The woman set her trap for women who gave birth to children they dared not acknowledge, but which they were not wicked enough to murder outright.

She wrote always in the vein of a kindly, lonely Christian woman, and as a rule her reward was $50 and the clothes of the child, to which she promised to be a mother, and which she usually dispatched as soon as it was in her clutches. She was bold to the point of madness in disposing of the bodies, and it is that among other things which suggest abnormal mental development which enabled her to gratify a desire to kill as well as a wish to grow rich by her fiendish occupation. Mrs. Dyer has been accused of child murder four times during her life, but on previous occasions proof was wanting.

The Huddlersfield Chronicle and West Yorkshire Advertiser

Thursday, June 11, 1896

EXECUTION OF MRS. DYER

On Wednesday morning, Mrs. Amelia Annie Dyer was executed in Newgate Gaol for the murder of two infant children committed to her charge. During her incarceration, the condemned woman, who was 57 years of age, has been a source of considerable trouble to the gaol officials on account of the very careful watching she needed to prevent the possibility of her destroying herself. Her behavior in the cell was most peculiar. She sat for hours with her eyes rivetted first on one of her attendants and then on the other, without speaking or betraying any emotion. She manifested such a dislike to one of her attendants that another had to take her place. The convict was not heard to utter one prayer in her cell by her attendants. In a letter she wrote to her daughter, Mrs. Palmer, last week, she said, "I have no soul. My soul was hammered out of me atnd Gloucester Asylum." Her thoughts were concentrated not on herself, but on her daughter. The latter was permitted to visit her on Friday morning last. The condemned woman received daily the attention of the prison chaplain, who did his best to prepare her for the end. She, however, maintained all along the stolid demeanor shown at the trial.

In order to spare Dyer the pain and mental anguish of remaining within hearing of the passing bell when Fowler, Milson, and Seaman were executed on Tuesday morning, the authorities arranged to remove her from Newgate to Holloway Gaol early. She was removed in the prison van, all the female officers in attendance upon her accompanying her. On the receipt of the telegram forwarded after the graves of the murderers executed in the morning had been filled in and paved, she was taken back to Newgate. Before reaching her cell she had to walk over the newly made graves.

Ms. Dyer retired to rest at the usual time of Tuesday night. She was in a wretched and agitated state of mind, and passed a very restless night.

The chaplain was in attendance early on Wednesday morning, and he spent most of the time that remained to the unhappy woman in her cell. The convict seemed in a dazed condition, and had to be supported whilst Billington performed the operation of pinioning her arms, which was done in a cell a very few paces from the scaffold. The distance to be traversed to the drop was only a few yards. The female officers proceeded with the wretched woman as far as the door of the scaffold shed, bade her farewell, and their gruesome duty ended, retired. The convict was quickly placed in the position beneath the beam, and the noose and cap were at once adjusted by Billington, his assistant rapidly performing the other preparations, the convict being meanwhile supported by the warders. The hangman pulled the lever, the drop fell without any hitch, and the wretched woman died instantly. Mrs. Dyer weighed 15 stone, and was given a drop of about 5 feet.

The Under-Sheriff Ruston informed a press representative, in an interview in the gaol immediately after the execution, that when asked by the governor of the prison at the last moment whether she had anything to say, Mrs. Dyer replied, "No sir, I have nothing whatever to say." She was very collected, and thanked the governor and the female warders for their kindness to her. The shortest route possible was taken to the scaffold. There was not a move of her body when the drop fell. Death was instantaneous, the execution being carried out in every respect satisfactorily.

The inquest on the body of Mrs. Dyer was, in accordance with the regulations, held at the Old Bailey two hours after the execution. The jury at once proceeded to view the body, which was lying across the drop in a shell. The features of the woman were perfectly calm and peaceful, and did not reveal the slightest signs of distortion beyond a swelling of the neck. Lieutenant-Colonel Milman, Governor of Newgate, was the first witness examined. He produced the death warrant, and testified that the execution was satisfactorily carried out in accordance with the law. Dr. James Scott, the medical officer attached to Newgate, deposed that he was present at the execution that morning, and it was expeditiously and properly conducted. Death, which was instantaneous, was caused by fracture and dislocation of the neck. The jury returned a verdict accordingly.

The contents of number 45, Kensington-road, the Reading residence of the late Mrs. Dyer, were sold by auction on Wednesday afternoon, and realized about 7 pounds 15 shilling. Some thousands of people watched the proceedings, a large number of women being present. Among the lots disposed of were the quilt on which the wretched woman was at work when arrested. A child's cradle, in which so many of her victims had slept, and an armchair made by Palmer, her son-in-law.

The Guardian

Saturday, January 17, 1903

THE BABY FARMING CASE
SENTENCES OF DEATH

At the Old Bailey, London, yesterday, before Mr. Justice Darling, the trial concluded of Annie Walters, aged 50, nurse, and Amelia Sach, 30, midwife, on an indictment charging them – Walters with the murder of a male child and Sach as an accessory before the fact of the alleged crime. The latter prisoner kept a nursing home at Claymore House, East Finchley, and it is alleged received money to provide a home for the child of Ada Galley, a domestic servant, who was confined in the home, and whose child, it was alleged, Walters took away and murdered. For the defense it was denied that there was any foundation for the suggestions of the prosecution that children were illegally disposed of at Claymore House. In summing up the Judge said the prisoners were not charged with keeping this home but with the crime of murder. The jury, therefore, would banish from their minds all feelings in respect of the character of the business. The main question was did Walters commit murder and was Sach a party to it. The Judge, who queried was it possible, in view of the facts, that the jury could acquit of criminal intent in the administration of the chlorodyne, refused to put the question of manslaughter to the jury at the request of the prisoners' counsel, remarked that he felt it was a question of murder simply.

After 40 minutes deliberation, the jury found both prisoners guilty, with a recommendation to mercy on account of their sex. Mr. Stephenson, for the prisoners, asked the court to reverse the case for the consideration of the High Court on the question of the admissibility of the evidence of a witness named Harris, and the judge said he could not do this.

Asked whether they had anything to say why sentence should not be passed, both prisoners replied no.

Mr. Justice Darling: Annie Walters and Amelia Sach, the jury has come to the only conclusions which, in my opinion, it was possible for them to come in your case. They have found you each guilty of the murder of that male child. It is plain to me that you have been the instigator of the other woman in the actual taking away of life as part of the business you carried on. You were in the habit, I am satisfied, of receiving these children from mothers and of obtaining money from them on the pretext that they would be adopted by people. You got the money for your own use and purposes, and then handed the children over to be done to death as rapidly as was consistent with no trail being left to bring you and your accomplice to justice. The jury has recommended you to mercy, but their reason is such that I implore you both to build little or no hope upon it. I have only now to pass the sentence of the law, and on my own behalf I ask you during the short time that life will remain to you to make your peace with God you have to meet.

Sentence of death was then passed.

Sach: I am innocent.

Walters: I never killed the baby.

The Anse Sentinel

Saturday, February 14, 1903

WOMEN HANGED.

London, Feb. 4.

Amelia Sach and Annie Walters, "baby farmers," were hanged at Holloway jail Tuesday. The women walked to the scaffold unaided and displayed remarkable fortitude. No woman had previously been hanged in England since March, 1900.

THE HORROR OF LYNCHINGS

AUTHOR'S COMMENTARY

Lynching, by definition, is murder committed by a mob outside of the law. Sadly, primarily in the southern states, for generations of African Americans lynching was a substantial and realistic fear. In the vast majority of cases, "negroes" were summarily hung by white mobs enraged by either real crimes or "alleged" crimes they were to have committed against white women.

History has demonstrated there were a number of societal issues that drove this conduct. After the Civil War, many believed the free black slaves were the cause of the financial difficulties in the South, and of course, inherent racism played a significant role in that perspective.

Spanning the years of 1882 to 1968, the NAACP, The National Archives and Records Administration, and other organizations have documented nearly 4,800 lynchings of "negroes" in the United States. Blacks were the victims almost seventy-five percent of the time, while lynching of whites accounted for roughly twenty-five percent.

The lynching of whites predominantly occurred in the West during the 1800s. Such crimes as murder, cattle rustling, horse thefts, rape of white women, and robbery saw many a man "strung up" by an inflamed mob. Ultimately, a number of the lynching victims would have been hung after due process of a legal trial but the fury of a mob intent on vigilante justice will never wait. Unfortunately, there are no accurate records regarding the number of whites lynched. Many victims were secretly taken into wooded areas, hung and their bodies left for scavengers. In some cases after the hanging, the bodies were buried in unmarked graves outside of cemeteries to be lost for all time.

There is a fact seldom discussed, and that was the practice of the lynching of "negroes" by "negroes." It was not common practice, but it did occur. And it happened for some of the same reasons.

The following stories are representative of whites lynching "negroes," and "negroes" lynching "negroes." Both are a shameful stain on the fabric of America's history.

We can only wonder how many innocent men, women, and children were lynched without merit.

Springville Journal

Thursday, September 21, 1893

NEGROES HANGED.

THREE BROTHERS STRUNG UP BY A MOB.

Brothers of Judge Estopinal's Slayer and Were Shielding the Murderer—Remained

Faithful to Their Brother Even

on the Scaffold—A Negro Boy Kicked to Death.

NEW ORLEANS, Sept. 18.

There was a triple lynching almost within the shadow of the city, but it was conducted so quietly that the account of the horrible affair was a surprise to the community.

The victims of the vengeance of the mob were three negro brothers named Julian and the crime which they expiated is so summary a manner was the shielding of a fourth brother, Roselius Julian, who on Friday afternoon shot Judge Victor Estopinal to death while the latter was trying him for a trivial offense seriously wounded the judge's son and then made good his escape.

In the pursuit made by the different posses during the day great lack of system was everywhere demonstrated. They were continually upon one another's trail and very many of them becoming disgusted with the aimless manner in which the hunt was being engineered came in and refused to further participate in the chase.

Towards nightfall the men who had been out manhunting all day and having met with no success, though they had frequently been sent on wild goose chases, began to grow fretful, and as the darkness thickened around them there fretfulness grew into desperation and they determined to do something to compel the relatives of the fugitive to disclose his whereabouts.

About 11 o'clock a body consisting of about 25 men, some armed with rifles and shotguns, came up to the jail and lit a lantern. They unlocked the door and then held a conference among themselves as to what they should do. Some were in favor of hanging the whole five, while others raised objections and insisted that only two of the brothers, Valsin and Bakile, should be taken out and strung up. This was finally agreed to and several of the men went into the jail and brought out the two doomed negroes.

They were hurried to a pasture 100 yards distance and there asked to take their last chance of saving their lives by making a confession. The negroes made no reply. They were then told to kneel down and pray. One did so, the other remained standing, but both prayed fervently. The taller negro was then hoisted up. He remained hanging fully five minutes before the second one was hanged.

The shorter negro stood gazing at the horrible death of his brother without flinching. The mob remained at the place for about half an hour when someone suggested that they go back and hang the other three. This was opposed by several, and it was finally decided that they should go back and take the remaining brother out to Camp Parapet and hang him there. The other two were to be taken out and flogged, with an order to get out of the parish in less than half an hour. The mob then started back to the jail to put their threats into execution. The third brother, Paul, was taken out to the camp, which is about a mile distant in the interior, and there he was hanged to a tree, his body hanging in full view of a morbid crowd during the day "as a warning to the negroes that they cannot go about killing white people," as one of the members of the mob put it.

In the meantime the real murderer is at liberty and his brothers, who died to save him from the fate which they met, will soon be resting in the unmarked graves, heroes of a peculiarly distinctive type.

During the search for Julian on Saturday one branch of the posse visited the house of a negro family in the neighborhood of Camp Parapet, and failing to find the object of their search tried to induce John Willis, a young negro, to disclose the whereabouts of Julian. He refused to do so, or could not do so, and was kicked to death by the gang.

NEGROES INTIMIDATED.

Prompt Action Prevented an Uprising to
Avenge the Triple Lynching.

NEW ORLEANS, Sept. 19.

Several negroes were seen in the neighborhood of Camp Parapet, armed with Winchesters. They made threats that they were going to be avenged for the lynching of their three comrades on Saturday. This was immediately communicated to the leading men of the parish, who sent out couriers and soon had gathered quite a small army. A squad of 40 men were left in the camp and the other men were distributed in squads from 5 to 15 men, all along the river front at intervals of half a mile, and on all the roads leading into the interior.

These men were kept on duty all night. Two squads of mounted police from the city were sent to the rescue and made the round of the parish.

The negroes disappeared as if they had been swallowed up by the earth. Not a single negro was seen throughout the night and this gives the impression that they are congregating at some place in the interior unknown to the whites.

Posses are still scouring the woods for the negro Roselieus Julian, but he seems to have been successful in eluding them.

Times Herald

Saturday, October 4, 1919

Editorial

LYNCHING OF NEGROES

Lynching negroes is fashionable sport in some parts of the country. Whenever a colored man commits a serious crime – sometimes when it is not so serious – he is strung up. But rarely is a white man lynched, no matter what he does. His case is permitted to take its course in the courts; but the mob summarily punishes the offending black, contrary to the Constitution of the United States and all legal procedure.

And yet the law of the land is the same for the black man as it is for the white man. They stand as equals before it. The one has just as good right to be tried in the courts as the other, but the mob will not have it that way. It usurps the functions of the courts and outrages the law, because it is violently prejudiced against the man who wears a black skin. It is actuated solely by race hatred.

The remedy is, of course, to punish the mob, but this is often a difficult thing to do. But it ought to be done, and until it is done, the habit of lynching colored men, and even colored women, will continue. You cannot reason the lynching passion out of human beings and whose bosoms it is by instinct aflame. Sterner methods must be employed.

Lynching is a despicable and inhuman crime and we have no respect for the man who engages in it. He is no better than any other murderer. The mark of Cain is on his forehead and he will wear it there on Judgment Day. Furthermore, no right thinking, properly civilized man or woman would have a hand in such disgraceful and un-Christian business as lynching a fellow mortal, black or white. Decent people do not usurp the functions of a public executioner.

AUTHOR'S COMMENTARY

The following article is from one newspaper providing a list of lynchings by date. The complete listing was very lengthy. I elected to only include a short sample of the list illustrating how commonplace lynchings were at the time.

Buffalo Weekly Express

Thursday, December 30, 1897

June 12 –In Kemper County, Mississippi, Sibley, negro, killed two negro women and three children while drunk, lynched by a mob of negroes.

Aug. 7 – Near Edna, Ga., Benjamin Mayfield, negro, accused of assault on a woman, was lynched.

Aug. 7 – Near Glenwood, Ga., Nat Mason, negro, accused of assault on a white woman, was shot to death by a mob.

Aug. 7 – At Nacogdoches, Tex., Essek White, negro, accused of assault on a white woman, was taken from jail and lynched.

Aug. 8 – At Brunswick, Miss., John Gordon, negro, was lynched for murder.

Aug. 14 – In the Chickamauga National Park, Tenn., an unknown white man was lynched for assault on a 13-year-old girl.

Aug. 17 – Near Asheville, N. C., Bob Brackett, negro, was lynched for assault on a white woman.

Aug. 19 – In Cook County, Ill., an unknown white man was shot to death by a mob of farmers for assault on a woman.

Aug. 21 – At Williamsburg, Ky., Elcany Sullivan, convicted of assault on a woman and sentenced to 20 years imprisonment, was taken from jail and hanged by a mob.

Aug. 22 – At Lovett, Ga., Andrew Green, negro, shot a white man and was pursued and lynched.

Aug. 23 – Near Anderson, Ark., Wiley Douglass, negro, was taken from officers and lynched. He was accused of killing a white man at a negro dance.

Aug. 26 – At Belleville, Tex., negro named Bonner, accused of assault on a woman, was taken from jail and lynched.

Aug. 26 – At Mooreville, Tex., Wiley Johnson, negro was lynched for attempting an assault on a white woman.

Aug. 26 – At Claiborne, Ala., Jack Pharr, negro, killed a white man who caught him robbing his safe, was taken from officers by a mob and lynched.

Sept. 6 – At Friends Mission, Va., Henry Wall, white, was lynched for assault and murder of a white girl. Later evidence showed that he probably was innocent.

Sept. 12 – In Macon, Ga., Charley Gibson, negro, killed another negro in a fight, was himself shot by officers and then lynched by a mob, which secured a confession that he had recently assaulted a white woman.

Chattanooga Daily Times

Friday, August 24, 1906

Negroes Arraying Themselves Against the Criminals of Their Race

FROM THE CHICAGO RECORD-HERALD

Midsummer is usually the time when lynchings of negroes are most frequent. Western lynchings and Eastern lynchings show no variation with the seasons, but in the South when June and July come there is a sharp increase. Statistics for many years show indeed that almost 50 percent more lynchings occur in these months than in the run of other months.

In August there is usually a falling off, which some students explain as a result of the camp meetings which are held in that month and which keep negroes too busy to have time for crimes. This year the August lynchings have been more numerous, and some of them have been of the spectacular character that attracts wide attention.

But more significant than the lynchings has been the attitude which the negroes themselves have been taking toward them. Instead of those tales of race war that sometimes come to us, we have seen negroes participating in lynchings, passing resolutions of approval, and even forming organizations, if not for lynching purposes, at least for the apprehension and punishment of members of their own race.

It was set in Columbia, S. C., a week or two ago, that a negro woman fired the first shot at a man who was lynched for crimes committed both against whites and against blacks. After the lynching, when the governor of the state was endeavoring to bring the members of the mob to punishment, the negro residents, or some of them, held a meeting and passed resolutions addressed to the whites which read: "We are with you, and if anything so serious as this you have our assistance in what you think best."

More striking still was the organization of colored farmers which held a convention at Houston, Tex., in July, and appointed vigilance committees for different sections of the state. In fourteen months, there have been seventy-three cases of criminal assault committed by negroes in Texas, and the better members of the race determined to stop it. This organization is hardly in working order as yet, but it is not impossible that from it a negro constabulary has been organized with excellent results in Jamaica.

There is no doubt that, if law-abiding negroes join in enforcing the law against criminals of their own race, there will soon be less race hatred excited by negro crimes and more probably that the law will be allowed to take its course. In the way the courts have been working in the south in the last year there is little reason for laying stress on the delays of justice, which formerly were so apt to result in the escape of offenders from punishment.

Staunton Spectator

Wednesday, July 6, 1892

Editorial

Negroes Lynching Negroes.

On last Wednesday night, in Wynn, Cass County, Ark., the negroes lynched a young negro who had outraged a negro girl.

On Thursday night there was a similar case at Haynes, Lee County, in the same state, when three hundred negroes took a negro named Donnelly from his cell and lynched him, hanging him to the limb of a tree. Tuesday Donnelly committed a felonious assault on a colored girl 12 years of age, living on the Campson plantation. The mob was composed entirely of colored people.

That is a crime for which both races in all sections of the country will lynch the perpetrator. What will the Republicans of the north have to say about these and similar cases? Both white and colored Republicans in the North have had a great deal to say in condemnation of the Southern people for lynching negroes for outraging white women. They are trying to make political capital out of it in the North, but they do the same thing when such crimes are committed in that part of the union.

Some of the negroes in the South have been making the same complaint of the whites for lynching negroes for this crime, but they do the same thing when the crime referred to is *committed on persons of their race, and it is to their credit that they do so, and their conduct is a vindication of the whites, and shows the injustice of their complaints. Instead of complaining and condemning, they should approve and endorse them, for their own conduct shows that they feel they did right. But for political capital, no such complaints would be made.*

THE CRIME OF BEING A WITCH

AUTHOR'S COMMENTARY

The Salem, Massachusetts, witch trials are a haunting reminder of an ignorant America. In a roughly two-year span from 1692-1693, over two hundred people faced a "jury or tribunal" of their community members on charges of practicing the "Devil's Magic," commonly known as witchcraft.

Most of the "witches" were women and, in the end, records indicate as many as twenty were ultimately executed for the fallacious crime.

History indicates the colonies eventually concluded the trials were a mistake and, in some cases, provided small compensation to the families of the executed.

The belief in witches still persists in parts of America and throughout the world.

Definition of words used in the following articles:

- An *auto-de-fé* was the ritual of public penance of condemned heretics and apostates. In this case, burning them alive was the punishment.

- *Ill Usage* was defined as bad or cruel treatment.

- Exhorteth is a 15th Century coinage meaning "to incite."

The words in the stories are not misspelled. I wrote the words as they appear in the articles. During the 1700s, it was not uncommon for people to spell the same word in a variety of configurations. The spellings make for slow reading, but they provide a glimpse into 17th Century reporting.

The Public Ledger

Thursday, February 7, 1760

Libson. Yesterday we had an auto de fe, at which we burned three young women that were heretics, one of them of exquisite beauty; two Jews, and an old woman, convicted of being a witch: one of the friars, who attended this last, reports, that he saw the devil fly out of her at the flake in the shape of a flame of fire. The populace behaved on this occasion with great good humour and sincere devotion.

Jacksons Oxford Journal

Saturday, June 28, 1760

TUESDAY'S POST.

FOREIGN AFFAIRS.

Yesterday arrived two Mails from FLANDERS.

Vienna, (Capital of Austria) June 7.

(Price two pence and halfpenny)

Lucifer, June 14.

They write from Glen in this Country, that on Wednesday se'nnight last, a Dispute arose between two old Women of that Town, one of whom calling the other a Witch, and the affirming, that she was no more a Witch than herself, a Challenge ensued, and they both agreed to be dipt by way of Trial; they accordingly stript to their Shifts, had their Thumbs and Great Toes tied across, and with a Cart Rope about their Middle, suffered themselves to be thrown into a Pool of Water; one of them is said to have sunk, whilst the other continued struggling upon the Surface, which the mob called Swimming, and deemed her infallible Sign of her being a Witch, insisting upon her impeaching her Accomplices in the Craft; she accordingly told them that in the neighbouring Village of Burton, there were several other old Women as much Witches is as she was: Their suspicions being confirmed by a Student in Astrology, or White-witch, who was referred to on account of a young Woman, said to be afflicted with an uncommon Disorder, and pronounced to be bewitched; the Mob in consequence of this Intelligence, on Thursday repaired to Burton, and after a little Consultation they proceeded to the old Woman's House on whom they had fixed the strongest suspicion; the poor old Creature on their Approach, locked the Door and went into a Chamber, and from the Window asked what they wanted?

They informed her that she was charged with being guilty of Witchcraft, which they were come to try her for, by Ducking; remonstrating at the same Time upon the Necessity there was of her giving this Proof whether she was a Witch or no; but upon her persisting in a positive Refusal to come down, they broke open the House, went into the Chamber, carried her down Stairs, and by force took her to a deep Gravel Pit full of Water, tied her Thumbs and Toes as above, then threw her in, where they kept her during Pleasure. The same Day the Mob tried the Experiment upon another poor old Woman, and on Thursday the third underwent a like Discipline.

Several of the Ringleaders in this Riot, we hear have been apprehended and carried before a Justice; two of which have been bound over to the Sessions, and others ordered to pay small Fines.

We shall just beg Leave, by Way of Admonition, to remind the Persons active in discovering who are Witches (and which we hope may be a Means of preventing the farther

Trial of this dangerous Experiment) to observe to them, that no longer ago than the Year 1751, at Tring in Hertfordshire, a Mob were determined to try by Ducking whether or not one Mrs. Osborne and her husband were Witches, (two poor harmless People, aged above 70) who accordingly tied as above, thrown into a muddy Pond, where after much Ducking and ill Usage, the old Woman was taken out, laid naked on the Bank, and died in a few Minutes; the poor Man who also used so cruelly that in a few Hours after he also died. The Coroner's Inquest brought in their Verdict Wilful Murder against nine of the Persons, specified; and 20 others whose Names were unknown. Thomas Colley one of these Rioters was brought to Trial, condemn'd, executed, and afterwards hanged in Chains. At the Place of Execution he signed a solemn Declaration relating to his Faith on Witchcraft, which was read at his Request and was as follows:

Good people!

I beseech you all to take Warning by an unhappy Man's suffering; that you be not deluded into so absurd and wicked a Conceit, as to believe that there are any such Beings upon Earth as Witches.

It was that foolish and vain Imagination, heighten'd and inflamed by the Strength of Liquor, which prompted me to be instrumental (with others as mad-brain'd as myself) in the horrid and barbarous Murder of Ruth Osborne, the supposed Witch, for which I am to deservedly to suffer Death.

I am fully convinced of my former Error, and with the sincerity of a dying Man, declare, that I do not believe there is such a Thing in being as a Witch; and pray God that none of you, tho' a contrary Perfusion, may hereafter be induced to think, that you have a Right in any shape to persecute, much less endanger the Life of a Fellow Creature.

I beg of you all, to pray to God to forgive me, and to wash clean my polluted Soul in the Blood of Jesus Christ, my Savior and Redeemer: so exhorteth you all, the dying.

Thomas Colley

THE OLD WEST

AUTHOR'S COMMENTARY

The Earp Family and Doc Holliday

For over a century, the adventures of the legendary Earp family have been extolled in all forms of media. Books, movies, and newspapers have all portrayed them as honorable lawmen bringing the worst desperadoes of the wild and wooly west to justice. No criminal could escape their grasp, and no person could escape their vengeance.

On October 26, 1881, in the dusty frontier mining town of Tombstone, Arizona, the Earp name became enshrined in the annals of history and folklore as the result of a gunfight at the O.K. Corral.

The longstanding hatred between the Earps (Wyatt, Morgan, and Virgil, and friend John H. "Doc" Holliday) and members of a cowboy gang had finally boiled over. The hostility erupted when the Earps and Holliday responded to the cowboys' threats to kill the Earps. The Earps acting as lawmen sought to disarm the gang, but it did not go well. It is unclear who shot first but, by the end, Tom and Frank McLaury and Billy Clanton were dead, and Ike Clanton had fled. The vendetta continued through 1882, killing Morgan and several others until Wyatt and Virgil left Arizona. The gunfight lasted only thirty seconds but became the most notorious and enduring story of the Wild West.

However, there is much more to the Earps' story. There were also more members of the Earps' immediate family whose story faded from history. Their back story is found in newspaper articles from the period. No books were written about their exploits until years after the O.K. Corral shootout. However, America's first crime reporters were on the story and, because of their work, we can travel back in time to within hours or days of the events and read their contemporary accounts. Without question, these are the best sources of information and prove to be the most accurate and exciting.

The Other Side of the Earps

From the reporters' accounts, Wyatt Earp and his brothers played both sides of the law. At times they served as law enforcement officers, while at other times they were thieves and bandits. According to media stories from the time, the best-known Earps were, as many others, a gang of criminals.

Wyatt's first recorded run-in with the law occurred in Fort Smith, Arkansas, in April 1871, when a grand jury indicted Wyatt Earp, Edward Kennedy, and John Shown for stealing horses in the Indian Territory. They stole two horses from Jim and William Keys, resulting in an arrest warrant being issued. On April 6, Deputy Marshal J.G. Owens arrested Wyatt and Kennedy in the Cherokee Nation; both posted a five hundred dollar bond and were released. Their trial was scheduled for November 13 at Fort Smith, but Wyatt jumped bail. The archives are not clear, but suggest Wyatt was eventually acquitted.

As you will note in the following newspaper accounts, the Earps' time in Tombstone, Arizona, praised their law enforcement efforts, which made them a legend. The accounts also exposed their hidden criminal activities.

There are last names in the articles which are spelled differently. This is how they were spelled in the original articles. I opted to keep the spelling as it appears to preserve the spirit of the stories. The articles also demonstrate how the news media then, like now, sometimes differed as to the facts. And remember, the life stories of Old West legends are never entirely accurate.

The Wichita Star

June 15, 1888

A FATAL LOVE

A STORY OF AN OLD-TIME WICHITA GIRL AND HOW SHE MET HER DEATH

For the Sake of the Love She Bore Her Desperado Lover

She Braves Her Family's Wrath and is Killed by Them—The Earps and Ike Clanton.

A little love story about former well-known Wichita people will undoubtedly prove of interest to all of the readers. The Earp family were well-known factors of this city a few years ago when the place was small and only a frontier town. Wyatt Earp was a police officer and enjoyed the reputation of being one of the most desperate men and the worst killer in the state.

He was a big fellow, with light hair and mustache and pale, almost white-looking eyes, but if he hated a man and glanced along the barrel of a gun his enemy's death warrant was usually signed.

The Earp family consisted of Virgil, Wyatt, Julian and Warren Earp, besides a beautiful sister named Jesse. The boys were all proud of their graceful, handsome and accomplished sister and sent her off to some of the best schools in the country to get her a first-class education. Before her schooling was completed, her father and brother had left Wichita and removed to Tombstone, Arizona, then the mecca of all desperate characters and there Miss Jesse rejoined her brother and father.

At this time, Wyatt Earp and Doc Halliday, also well known in Wichita, were the chiefs of the famous stage robber bands that infested that interesting country, while a great, large, handsome fellow, also a chief of a gang called the Rustlers, was named Ike Clanton.

Between the two parties, a deadly enmity existed, and between them they finally almost exterminated each other. In the fight between the two factions and in which battle shotguns were used, three members of the Clanton gang and Clanton's own brother were killed, while Warren Earp met his death, and the Earp faction getting worsted were compelled to flee the country, going to Gunnison, Colorado, and of course taking their beautiful sister with them. But previous to this fatal shooting in which so many desperados lost their lives, Ike Clanton had met Jesse Earp at a dance and had fallen passionately in love with her and she on her side had to return that love with equal fervor. It was a case of love at first sight on both sides.

As soon as the Earps heard that their sister loved their most deadly enemy there was trouble ahead. Virgil Earp wished to turn his sister out of house and home or else kill her, but Wyatt thought differently and said that she should be kept a prisoner until she had forgotten her handsome desperado lover.

A short time after the Earps had reached Gunnison and were as usual running the town with a high hand, their beautiful sister disappeared. A short investigation revealed the fact that she had fled with their worst hated foe Ike Clanton, who had at the risk of his life entered the town run by them and had carried off their sister. This was too much and there was mounting in hot haste and a pursuit was organized with the Earps, Doc Holliday and several other desperadoes as pursuers.

The lovers had a good start, but Clanton, brave man that he was, took all possible precautions to escape from them. Over pathless mountains among bears and all sorts of wild animals and poisonous reptiles the lovers fled for thirty-six hours, without food, until they finally when completely worn out reached San Miguel. Here are they rested and got something to eat, for they were famished. After recovering from their fatigue they sought out a minister and were married, but their happiness was short lived. Just as they emerged from the pastor's house they were sighted by the Earp gang who at once gave chase. Clanton was brave, but he knew that alone against that crowd he stood no show, so he caught his wife in his arms and running to a mine nearby sought and obtained protection from the miners who declared they would see fair play and that such a love match interested them.

At last it was arranged that a duel be fought with pistols between Julian Earp and Ike Clanton, and if Clanton won, he would go free. This being agreed to the men stationed themselves one hundred feet apart and began to shoot. Julian got the first shot, but missed when Clanton with a well-directed bullet severed his opponent's heart and the same minister that had married the sister a short time before read the funeral services over her brother the same day.

At this stage of the game, the Earps got in their strategic work. They pretended that the matter had been satisfactorily settled and rode back towards Gunnison, but not very far.

As soon as they were out of sight of the camp, they whirled around and struck the road ten miles beyond San Miguel where they soon found the tracks made by the horses ridden by Clanton and his bride. Following onto the next town they caught the people they were after at supper at a hotel and fired a volley at them through the window. Poor Jesse was hit, but her husband was not, and hastily picking up his fainting wife Clanton made for his horse and mounting rode off.

All night they roamed through the mountains the horrified husband doing all in his power to alleviate the suffering of the poor girl who had been shot by her own brother or by his comrade. The next morning, she died in her husband's arms and he determined to revenge her.

Two years later, Clanton killed Curly Bill, a cousin of the Earps and one of the pursuing party at Socorro, Mo. About a year ago, Birgit and Wyatt Earp met Clanton in Arizona and all began to shoot. Clinton was killed, but he wounded Wyatt Earp so badly that he is yet a cripple.

He is now the marshal at San Bernardino, California. He should make a good officer as it takes a thief to catch a thief.

The San Francisco Examiner

Sunday, August 2, 1896

How Wyatt Earp Routed a Gang of Arizona Outlaws

It may be that the trail of blood will seem to lie too thickly over the pages that I write. If I had it in me to invent a tale, I would fain lighten and the crimson stain so that it would glow no deeper than a demure pink. But half a lifetime on the frontier attunes a man's hand to the six-shooter rather than the pen, and it is lucky that I am asked only for facts, for more than facts I could not give.

Half a lifetime of such turbulent days and nights as we will never again be seen in this, or, I believe, in any land, might be expected to tangle a man's brain with memories none too easy to sift apart. But for the corner-stone of this episodic narrative I cannot make better choice than the bloody the feud in Tombstone, Ariz., which cost me a brave brother and cost more than one worthless life among the murderous dogs who pursued me and mine only less bitterly than I pursued them.

And so as I marshal my characters, my stalwart brothers, Virgil and Morgan, shall stand on the right of the stage with my dear old comrade, Doc Holliday; on the left shall be arrayed Ike Clanton, Sheriff Behan, Curley Bill and the rest. Fill in the stage with miners, gamblers, rustlers, stage robbers, murderers and cowboys, and the melodrama is ready to begin. Nor shall our heroin be wanting, for Big Nose Kate was shaped for the part both by nature and circumstances. Poor Kate! Frontier whiskey must have laid her low long since. And that gives me an opportunity to introduce the reader to both Doc Holliday and Kate by telling of an episode in their checkered lives two years before the action of my melodrama begins.

It happened in 77, when I was City Marshal of Dodge City, Kan. I had followed the trail of some cattle-thieves across the border into Texas, and during a short stay in Fort Griffin I first met Doc Holliday and the woman who was known variously as Big Nose Kate, Kate Fisher and, on occasions of ceremony, Mrs. Doc Holliday. Holliday asked me a good many questions about Dodge City and seemed inclined to go there, but before he had made up his mind about it my business called me over to Fort Clarke. It was while I was on my way back to Fort Griffin that my new friend and his Kate found it necessary to pull their stakes hurriedly. Whereof the plain, unvarnished facts are these;

Doc Holliday was spending the evening in the poker game, which was his custom whenever faro bank did not present superior claims on his attention. On his right sat Ed Bailey, who needs no description because he is soon to drop out of this narrative. The trouble began, as it was related to me afterward, by Ed Bailey monkeying with the deadwood, or what people who live in the cities call discards. Doc Holliday admonished him once or twice to "play poker"—which is your seasoned gambler's method of cautioning a friend to stop cheating, but the misguided Bailey persisted in his furtive actions to the deadwood. Finally, having detected him again, Holliday pulled down a pot without showing his hand, which he had a perfect right to do. Thereupon Bailey started to throw his gun around on Holliday, as might have been expected. But before he could pull the trigger Doc Holliday had jerked a knife out of his breast pocket and with one sideways swipe had caught Bailey just below the brisket.

Well, that broke up the game, and pretty soon Doc Holliday was sitting cheerfully in the front room of the hotel, guarded by the City Marshal and a couple of policemen, while a hundred miners and gamblers clamored for his blood. You see, he had not lived in Fort Griffin very long, while Ed Bailey was well-liked. It wasn't long before Big Nose Kate, who had a room downtown, heard about the trouble and went up to take a look at her Doc through a back window. What she saw and heard led her to think that his life wasn't worth ten minutes purchase, and I don't believe it was. There was a shed at the back of the lot, and a horse was stabled in it. She was a kind-hearted girl, was Kate, for she went to the trouble of leading the horse into the alley and tethering it there before she set fire to the shed. She almost got a six-shooter from a friend down the street, which, with the one she always carried, made two.

It all happened just as she had planned it. The shed blazed up and she hammered at the door, yelling "Fire!"

Everybody rushed out, except the Marshal, the constables and the prisoner. Kate walked in as bold as a lion, threw one of her six-shooters on the Marshal and handed the other to Doc Holliday.

"Come on, Doc," she said with a laugh.

He didn't need any second invitation, and the two of them backed out of the hotel, keeping the officers covered. All that night, they hid among the willows down by the creek, and early the next morning, a friend of Kate's brought them two horses and some of Doc Holliday's clothing from his room. Kate dressed up in a pair of pants, a pair of boots, a shirt, and a hat, and the pair of them got away safely and rode the 400 miles to Dodge City, where they were installed in great style when I got back home.

Which reminds me that during my absence, the man whom I had left behind as a deputy had been killed by some cowboys who are engaged in the fascinating recreation known as "shootin' up the town." This incident is merely mentioned as a further sign of the time, and as a further excuse for the blood which cannot but trickle through the web of my remembrance.

Such, then, was the beginning of my acquaintance with Doc Holliday, the mad, merry scamp with a heart of gold and nerves of steel who, in the dark years that followed, stood at my elbow in many a battle to the death. He was a dentist, but he preferred to be a gambler. He was a Virginian, but he preferred to be a frontiersman and a vagabond. He was a philosopher, but he preferred to be a wag. He was long, lean, and ash-blonde, and the quickest man with a six-shooter I ever knew. It wasn't long after I returned to Dodge City that his quickness saved my life. He saw a man draw on me behind my back. "Look out, Wyatt!" he shouted, while the words were coming out of his mouth he had jerked his pistol out of his pocket and shot the other fellow before the latter could fire.

On such incidents as that are built the friendships of the frontier.

In 1879, Dodge City was beginning to lose much of the snap, which had given it a charm to men of restless blood, and I decided to move to Tombstone, which is just building up a reputation. Doc Holliday thought he would move with me. Big Nose Kate had left him long before—they were always a quarrelsome couple—and settled in Las Vegas, N. M. He looked her up in route and the old tenderness reasserted itself, she resolved to through in her lot with his in Arizona. As for me, I was tired of the trials of a peace officer's life and wanted no more of it. But as luck would have it, I stopped at Prescott to see my brother Virgil, and there I met C. P. Dake, the United States Marshal of the Territory. Dake had heard of me before, and he begged me so hard to take the deputyship in Tombstone that I finally consented. It was thus that the real troubles of a lifetime began.

The boom had not struck Tombstone then, but it did a few months later, when the mills for treating the ore were completed, and the tales about the fabulous riches of the silver mines were bruited abroad. Before long the town had a population of 10,000 or 12,000, of whom about 300 were cattle-thieves, stage robbers, murderers and outlaws.

For the first eight months I worked as a shotgun messenger for Wales, Fargo and Co., and beyond the occasional excitement of an abortive holdup and a few excursions after cattle-thieves and homicides in my official capacity, everything was as quiet as the grave. Then the proprietors of "The Oriental," the biggest gambling-house in town, offered to take me into partnership. One of them, his name was Rickabaugh and he was a San Francisco man, was unpopular, and a coterie of the tough gamblers were trying to run the firm out of town. The proprietors had an idea that their troubles would cease if they had the Deputy United States Marshal for a partner, and so it proved, for a time at least. So I turned over my position with Wells, Fargo and Co. to my brother Morgan, who held it for six months, after which I gave him a job in "The Oriental." My brother Virgil had also joined me, and when the town was incorporated he was appointed Chief of Police.

About this time was laid the foundation of the vendetta which became the talk of the frontier and resulted in no end of bloodshed.

A band of rustlers held up the coach and killed the driver and one of the passengers. Virgil and I, with another man, followed them into the mountains for seventeen days, but our horses gave out and they got away from us. When we got back to town I went to Ike Clanton, who was a sort of leader among the rustlers, and offered to give him all the $6,000 reward offered by Wells, Fargo & Co. if he would lead me to where I could arrest the murderers. After thinking about it deeply he agreed to send a partner of his, named Joe Hill, to lead them from where they were hiding to someplace within twenty-five miles of Tombstone, where I could get them. But in case I killed his partners he wanted to be sure that the reward would be paid alive or dead. In order to assure him I got Wells Fargo's agent, Marshall Williams, to telegraph to San Francisco about it, and a reply came in the affirmative. So Clanton sent Hill off to decoy the men I wanted. That was to take several days, and in the meantime Marshall Williams got drunk, and, suspecting that I was using Ike Clanton for some purpose, tried to pump him about it. Clanton was terrified at the thought of any third person knowing of our bargain and accused me of having *told Williams. I denied it, and then he accused me of having told Doc Holliday. Fear and whiskey robbed Clanton of his discretion and he let out his secret to Holliday, who had known nothing about it. Doc Holliday, who was the soul of honor, berated him vigorously for his treachery, and the conversation was heard by several people.*

That was enough for Clanton. He knew that his only alternative was to kill us or be killed by his own people. Early next morning Virgil and I were told that he was out with a Winchester and a six-shooter looking for us. So we went out looking for him, taking different routes. Virgil was going down Fourth street when Clanton came out of the hallway, looking in an opposite direction. "I want you, Ike," said Virgil, walking up behind him. Clanton through his gun around and tried to take a shot, but Virgil knocked it away, pulled his own and arrested his man. Ike was fined $25 for disturbing the peace.

Ike Clanton's next move was to telegraph to Charleston, ten miles away, for Billy Clanton, Tom McLowery, Frank McLowery and Billy Clayton, hard men, every one. They came galloping into town, loaded up with ammunition and swearing to kill us off in short order. Thirty or forty citizens offered us their help, but we said we could manage the job alone. "What had we better do?" said Virgil. "Go and arrest 'em," said I.

The four newcomers and Ike Clanton stationed themselves on a fifteen-foot lot between two buildings in Fremont street and send us word that if we did not come down there and fight they would waylay and kill us. So we started down after them, Doc Holliday, Virgil, Morgan and I. As we came to the lot they moved back and got their backs against one of the buildings. "I'm going to arrest you, boys." said Virgil. For answer, their six-shooters began to spit. Frank McLowery fired at me and Billy Clanton at Morgan. Both missed. I had a gun in my overcoat pocket and I jerked it out at Frank McLowery, hitting him in the stomach. At the same time Morgan shot Billy Clanton in the breast. So far we had got the best of it, but just then Tom McLowery, who had got behind his horse, fired under the animal's neck and bored a hole right through Morgan sideways. The bullet entered one shoulder and came out the other.

"I've got it, Wyatt!" said Morgan.

"Then get behind me and keep quiet," I said—but he didn't.

By this time bullets are flying so fast that I could not keep track of them. Frank McLowery had given a yell when I shot him and made for the street, with his hand over his stomach. Ike Clanton and Billy Clanton were shooting fast, and so was Virgil, and the two latter made a break for the street. I fired a shot which hit Tom McLowery's horse and made it break away, and Doc Holliday took the opportunity to pump a charge of buckshot out of a Wells Fargo shotgun into Tom McLowery, who promptly fell dead. In the excitement of the moment Doc Holliday didn't know what he had done and flung away the shotgun in disgust, pulling his six-shooter instead.

Then I witnessed a strange spectacle. Frank McLowery and Billy Clanton were sitting in the middle of the street, both badly wounded, but emptying their six-shooters like lightning. One of them shot Virgil through the leg and he shot Billy Clanton. Then Frank McLowery started to his feet and struggled across the street, though he was full of bullets. On the way he came face-to-face with Doc Holliday. "I've got ye now, Doc," he said.

"Well, you're a good one if you have," said Doc Holliday, with a laugh. With that they both aimed. But before you can understand what happened next I must carry the narrative back half minute.

After the first exchange and the lot Ike Clanton had got into one of the buildings from the rear and when I reached the street he was shooting out of one of the front windows. Seeing him aim at Morgan I shouted: "Look out, Morg, you're getting it in the back!"

Morgan wheeled around and in doing so fell on his side. While in that position he caught sight of Doc Holliday and Frank McLowery aiming at each other. With a quick drop, he shot McLowery in the head. At the same instant McLowery's pistol flashed and Doc Holliday was shot in the hip.

That ended the fight. Ike Clanton and Billy Clanton ran off and made haste to give themselves up to the Sheriff, for the citizens were out a hundred strong to back us up.

I have described this battle with as much particularity as possible, partly because there are not many city dwellers who have more than a vague idea of what such a fight really means, and partly because I was rather curious to see how it would look in cold type. It may or may not surprise some readers to learn that from the first to the last shot fired not more than a minute elapsed.

Of the exciting events which followed I can give no more than a brief account. The principal factor in all that happened was Sheriff Johnny Behan, my political rival and personal enemy. Doc Holliday and I were arrested on a charge of murder. My two brothers were exempt from this proceeding because they were both disabled. We were acquitted at the preliminary hearing and rearrested on another warrant charging the same offense. This time the hearing was held at Contention, nine miles from Tombstone, and we would have been assassinated on the road had not a posse of the best citizens insisted on accompanying the Sheriff as a guard. The hearing was never completed, because Holliday and I were released on a writ of habeas corpus. In the meantime, the Grand Jury persistently refused to indict us.

But the determination to assassinate us never relaxed. Three months later Virgil was returning home to the hotel, and when he was halfway across the street five double-barreled shotguns were discharged at him from an ambuscade. One-shot shattered his left arm another passed through his body. I arrested several of the assassins, but twenty or thirty rustlers swore to an alibi and they were acquitted.

Three months later, before Virgil had recovered from his wounds, Morgan was shot dead through the glass door of a saloon, while he was playing a game of pool. I sent his body home to Colton, Cal., and shipped off Virgil—a physical wreck—on the same train from Tucson. But even at the depot I was forced to fight Ike Clanton and four or five of his friends who had followed us to do murder. One of them, named Frank Stilwell, who was believed to be Morgan's murderer, was killed by my gun going off when he grasped it. When I returned to Tombstone Sheriff Behan came to arrest me, but I refused to surrender, and he weakened. For a long time thereafter, I occupied the anomalous position of being a fugitive from the county authorities, and performing the duties of Deputy United States Marshal, with the sanction and moral support of my chief. With Doc Holliday and one of two faithful comrades I went into camp among the hills and withstood more than one attack from outlaws who had been implicated in the death of one brother and the disablement of another—attacks which resulted fatally to some of my enemies and left me without a scratch.

One such encounter I will describe because it illustrates as well as anything could some of the exigencies of a frontier vendetta.

We had ridden twenty-five miles over the mountains with the intention of camping at a certain spring. As we got near the place I had a presentiment that something was wrong, and unlimbered my shotgun. Sure enough, nine cowboys sprang up from the bank where the spring was and began firing at us. I jumped off my horse to return the fire, thinking my men would do the same, but they retreated. One of the cowboys, who is trying to pump some lead into me with a Winchester, was a fellow named Curly Bill, a stage-robber whom I had been after for eight months, and for whom I had a warrant in my pocket. I fired both barrels of my gun into him, blowing him all to pieces. With that the others jumped into a clump of willows and kept on firing, so I retreated, keeping behind my horse. He was a high-strung beast, and the firing frighten him so that whenever I tried to get my Winchester from the saddle he would rear up and keep it out of my reach. When I had backed out about a hundred yards I started to mount. Now, it was a hot day, and I had loosened my cartridge belt two or three holes. When I tried to get astride I found that it had fallen down over my thighs, keeping my legs together. While I was perched up thus, trying to pull my belt higher with one hand, the horn of the saddle was shot off. However, I got away all right, and just then my men rallied. But I did not care to go back at the rustlers, so we sought out another waterhole for camp. The skirt of my overcoat was shot to pieces on both sides, but not a bullet had touched me.

Sheriff Behan trailed us with a big posse composed of rustlers, but it was only a bluff, for when I left word for him where he could find us and waited for him to come he failed to appear.

My best friends advised me to leave the territory, so I crossed into Colorado. While I was there they tried to get a requisition for me, but the governor refused to sign it.

It's an old story now, I have been in Arizona of recent years, as near Tombstone as Tucson, in fact—but no one sought to molest me. The outlaws who were my worst enemies are mostly killed off or in the penitentiary. Poor Doc Holliday died of consumption three years ago in Colorado. My brother Virgil is running a stock ranch in Texas. A large section of his upper arm is entirely without bone, and yet he can use his fingers.

On reading it over it seems to me that there is not only too much blood, but too much of myself and my story. However, a man gets in the habit of thinking about himself when he spends half a lifetime on the frontier.

—Wyatt S. Earp

SHOOTOUT AT THE O.K. CORRAL

Arizona Weekly Citizen

Sunday, October 30, 1881

A DESPERATE STREET FIGHT

Marshal Virgil Earp, Morgan and Wyatt Earp and

Doc Holliday Meet the Cowboys—Three Men Killed and Two Wounded,

One Seriously—Origin of the Trouble and its Tragical Terminations

(Tombstone Nugget, Oct. 27)

The 26th October will always be marked as one of the crimson days in the annals of Tombstone, a day when blood flowed as water, and human life was held as a shuttlecock, a day always to be remembered as witnessing the bloodiest and deadliest street fight that has ever occurred in this place, or probably in the territory.

THE ORIGIN OF THE TROUBLE

Dates back to the first arrest of Stilwell and Spencer for the robbery of the Bisbee stage. The co-operation of the Earps with the sheriff and his deputies in the arrest causing a number of the cowboys to, it is said, threaten the lives of all interested in the capture. Still, nothing occurred to indicate that any such threats would be carried into execution. But Tuesday night Ike Clanton and Doc Holliday had some difficulty in the Alhambra saloon. Hard words passed between them, and when they parted it was generally understood that the feeling between the two men was that of intense hatred. Yesterday morning Clanton came on the street armed with a rifle and a revolver, but was almost immediately arrested by Marshal Earp, disarmed and fined by Justice Wallace for carrying concealed weapons. While in the courtroom Wyatt Earp told him that as he had made threats against his life he wanted him to make his fight, to say how, when and where he would fight, and to get his crowd, and he (Wyatt) would be on hand. In reply Clanton said:

FOUR FEET OF GROUND

Is enough for me to fight on, and I'll be there." A short time later this William Clanton and Frank McLowry came in town, and as Thomas McLowry was already here the feeling soon became general that a fight would ensue before the day was over and crowds of expectant men stood on the corner of Allen and Fourth streets awaiting the coming conflict.

It was now about two o'clock, and at this time Sheriff Behan appeared upon the scene and told Marshal Earp that if he disarmed his posse, composed of Morgan and Wyatt Earp, and Doc Holliday, he would go down to the O.K. Corral, where Ike and James Clanton and Frank and Tom McLowry were and disarmed them. The Marshal did not desire to do this until sure that there was no danger of an attack from the other party. The Sheriff went to the corral and told the cowboys that they must put their arms away and not have any trouble. Ike Clanton and Tom McLowry said they were not armed, and Frank McLowry said he would not lay his aside. In the meantime the Marshal had concluded to go and, if possible, end the matter by disarming them, and as he and his posse came down Fremont Street towards the corral, the sheriff stepped out and said, "HOLD UP BOYS, don't go down there or there will be trouble; I have been down there to disarm them." But they passed on, and when within a few feet of them the Marshal said to the Clanton's and McLowrys, "Throw up your hands, boys, I intend to disarm you." As he spoke Frank McLowry made a motion to draw his weapon, when Wyatt Earp pulled his and shot him, the ball striking on the right side of his abdomen. About the same time Doc Holliday shot Tom McLowry in the right side, using a short shotgun, such as is carried by Wells, Fargo & Co's., messengers. In the meantime Billy Clanton had shot at Morgan Earp, the ball passing through the point of the left shoulder blade across his back, just grazing the backbone and coming out at the shoulder, the ball remaining inside of his shirt. He fell to the ground, but in an instant gathered himself, and raising in a sitting position fired at Frank McLowry as he crossed Fremont street, and at the same instant Doc Holliday shot at him, both balls taking effect, either of which would have proved fatal, as one struck him in the right temple and the other in the left breast. As he started across the street, however, he pulled his gun down on Holliday saying, "I've got you now."

"Blaze away! You're a Daisy if you have," replied Doc. This shot of McLowry's passing through Holliday's pistol pocket, just grazing the skin. While this was going on Billy Clanton had shot Virgil Earp in the right leg, the ball passing through the calf, inflicting a severe flesh wound. In turn he had been shot by Morg Earp in the right side of the abdomen, and twice by Virgil or, once in the right wrist and once in the left breast. Soon after the shooting commenced Ike Clanton ran through the O.K. Corral, crossed Allen Street into Kellogg's saloon, and thence into Toughnut Street, where he was arrested and taken to the county jail.

The firing altogether did not occupy more than twenty-five seconds, during which time fully thirty shots were fired. After the fight was over Billy Clanton, who, with wonderful vitality, survived his wounds for fully an hour, was carried by the editor and foreman of the Nugget into a house near where he lay, and everything possible done to make his last moments easy. He was "game" to the last, never uttering a word of complaint, and just before breathing his last he said, "Goodbye, boys; go away and let me die." The wounded were taken to their houses, and at three o'clock this morning were resting comfortably. The dead bodies were taken in charge by the Coroner and an inquest will be held upon them at 10 o'clock to-day. Upon the person of Thomas McLowry was found between $300 and $400, and checks and certificates of deposit to the amount of nearly $3000.

DURING THE SHOOTING, Sheriff Behan was standing nearby commanding the contestants to cease firing but was powerless to prevent it. Several parties who were in the vicinity of the shooting had narrow escapes from being shot. One man who had lately arrived from the East had a ball pass through his pants. He left for home this morning. A person called "the Kid," who shot Hicks at Charleston recently, was also grazed by a ball. When the Vizina whistle gave the signal that there was a conflict between the officers and the cowboys, the mines on the hill shut down and the miners were brought to the surface. From the Contention mine a number of men, fully armed, were sent to the town in a four-horse carriage. At the request of the sheriff the "vigilantes," or Committee of Safety, are called from the streets by a few sharp toots from the Vizina whistle.

During the early part of the evening there was a strong rumor that a mob would attempt to take Ike Clanton from the jail and lynch him, and prevent any such unlawful proceedings a strong guard of deputies was placed around that building, and will be so continued until all danger is past. At 8 o'clock last evening, Finn Clanton, a brother of Billy and Ike, came in town, and placing himself under the guard of the sheriff, visited the morgue to see the remains of one brother, and then passed the night in jail and company with the other.

OMINOUS SOUNDS.

Shortly after the shooting ceased the whistle at the Vizina mine sounded a few short toots, and almost simultaneously a large number of citizens appeared on the streets, armed with rifles and a belt of cartridges around their waists. These men formed in line and offered their services to the peace officers to preserve order, in case any attempt at disturbance was made, or any interference offered to the authorities of the law. However, no hostile move was made by anyone, and quiet and order was fully restored, and in a short time the excitement died away.

AT THE MORGUE.

The bodies of the three slain cowboys lay side by side, covered with a sheet. Very little blood appeared on their clothing, and only on the face of young Billy Clanton was there any distortion of the features or evidence of pain in dying. The features of the two McLowry boys looked as calm and placid in death, as if they had died peaceably, surrounded by loving friends and sorrowing relatives. No unkind remarks were made by anyone, but a feeling of unusual sorrow seemed to prevail at the sad occurrence. Of the McLowry brothers we could learn nothing of their previous history before coming to Arizona. The two brothers owned quite an extensive ranch on the lower San Pedro, some seventy or eighty miles from the city, to which they had removed their band of cattle since the recent Mexican and Indian troubles. They did not bear the reputation of being of a quarrelsome disposition, but were known as fighting men, and have generally conducted themselves in a quiet and orderly manner when in Tombstone.

AUTHOR'S COMMENTARY

Approximately a month after the deadly shootout at the O.K. Corral, John P. Gosper, Acting Governor of the Arizona Territory, visited Tombstone and the surrounding area in an attempt to understand the cause of lawlessness in the region. Below is his private letter to Crawley P. Dake, the US Marshal for the Arizona Territory. It provides an additional perspective of Tombstone from a senior person within the government.

During the 1880s in Tombstone and other regions of the west, "Cow Boy" was two words, and labeling someone as such was considered an insult, as the term was used to describe horse thieves, bandits, and other outlaws.

Office of the Executive

Prescott, A.T. Nov. 28th, 1881

Hon. D. P. Dake

U.S. Marshal.

Dear Sir,

In reply to your communication of this date asking me to give you my opinion of the causes of the frequent disturbances of the public peace at Tombstone and vicinity in this territory, with such suggestions as might occur to me looking to a remedy for the unfortunate occurrences, based upon facts obtained by me on my recent visit to that section.

Permit me to say, that the underlying cause of all the disturbances of the peace, and the taking of property unlawfully, is the fact that all men of every shade of character in that new and rapidly developed section of mineral wealth, in their mad career after money, have grossly neglected local self-government, until the more lazy and lawless elements of society have undertaken to prey upon the more industrious and honorable classes for their subsistence and gains.

The civil officers of the County of Cochise and City of Tombstone, partaking of the general reckless spirit of rapid accumulation of money and property, is another of public disturbances, and as much as they have sinned to "wink at crime" and you have neglected a prompt discharge of duty, for the hope and sake of gain.

The thoroughly abandoned class of men called highway robbers and cattle thieves called "Cow Boys" cunningly taking advantage of the favorable state of affairs for themselves, have robbed from the wealthier class of citizens and when apprehended or detected by the officers of the law, have in many cases, no doubt, purchased their liberty, or have paid well to be left unmolested.

The peaceful and law-abiding citizens of the section of the territory above named are very generally of the opinion that the officers of the law are often themselves in league with the "Cow Boy" element to obtain illegal gains.

Another cause of the troubles alluded to is the fact that the present sheriff of Cochise County and one of the Earp brothers, not your deputy, but a brother to the latter being in some manner connected with the police force for the City of Tombstone, are candidates or applicants for the sheriffship at the polls in another season, the rivalry between them having extended into a strife to secure influence and aid from all quarters has lead them and the particular friends of each to sins of commission and omission greatly at cost of peace and prosperity.

The two newspapers published in Tombstone, are also censorable for the course they have pursued in relations to public and private matters.

In the strife and jealousies between the Sheriff and his Deputies of the County, and the City Marshal, the two papers have taken sides very largely through selfish motives of gain, – the County patronage being given to one of the papers for its hearty support and the City patronage to the other for its support.

Still another cause of the general lawlessness prevailing in that section of our Territory, is the fact that many citizens are dealing dishonestly with one hand secretly behind them, handling the stolen property of the "Cow Boys," while with the other hand openly before them they are disposing of the stolen property (mostly beef cattle) to honest citizens. Afterwards dividing with the regular thieves.

This class of criminal is the most difficult to reach and bring to justice. Hotels, saloons, restaurants, etc., where the rough "Cow Boy" element spend their money freely, are both weak and wicked in their sympathy for and protection of this lawless class.

From my last visit to Tombstone and vicinity, since the killing of the McLowery boys, and Clanton in the streets of Tombstone by the Earps, I gather the above, and many other facts and beliefs.

Now as to the remedy to be applied, I would suggest, that the Department of Justice in which you are serving be requested to furnish you with funds sufficient to enable you to employ a man of well-known courage and character of cool sound judgment, which your good judgment can secure. Who, with a suitable posse of men, can first fully comprehend the true nature of the situation, and then with proper discretion and courage, go forward with a firm and steady hand bringing as rapidly as possible the leading spirits of this lawless class to a severe and speedy punishment.

It might be a wise and successful measure for the Executive of the Territory to cause the removal from office of the sheriff while yourself as US Marshal be able likewise in securing deputies of the end that men possessing the confidence of the public, and who would work in harmony with each other in enforcing the law and keeping the peace, could be appointed.

At present however, I do not think it would be prudent for me, as acting Governor to resort to measures of that character.

Simply as acting Governor, I am not assured the time it would require to inaugurate and carry through the extreme or radical measures the situation certainly requires.

Hoping the knowledge and suggestions given above, may become available to you in the matter of bringing about a better state of affairs, and pledging you all the aid and support possible to be given from this Department.

I am most Respectively

Your obedient servant

John P. Gosper Acting Governor

San Francisco Chronicle

Monday, July 9, 1900

WARREN EARP SHOT DOWN

KILLED IN SALOON BRAWL AT WILLCOX

A MAN WHO HE HAD BULLIED

FOR MONTHS ENDS HIS CAREER

The Story of the Gang Which Was Once the Terror of Tombstone and the Cattle Rustlers.

Special Dispatch to the "Chronicle."

WILLCOX (A. T.), July 7.

Warren Earp, the youngest of the four brothers, whose names twenty years ago were synonymous with gunfighting on the Arizona frontier, "died with his boots on" here yesterday. He was shot through the heart in a saloon by Cowboy Johnny Boyett, and died almost instantly.

The shooting occurred early in the morning and grew out of the feud that had existed between the two men ever since the bloody fights between the Earps and the Arizona cattle rustlers about Tombstone in the early eighties. Earp had habitually bullied Boyett for months past, and the latter always tried to avoid a quarrel. A few days ago Earp cornered Boyett in a saloon, and, pressing of a revolver against Boyett's stomach, made him promise that if they ever quarreled again the one should kill the other.

The two men met in a restaurant and Earp began his abuse. Boyett went into an adjoining saloon, followed by Earp. The latter said, "Boyett, go get your gun and we'll settle the matter right here. I've got my gun; go get yours."

Boyett was willing and agreed to return in a few moments and fight it out. Earp also left the saloon. Boyett return very soon and finding Earp gone warned all loungers in the saloon to clear out, emphasizing his warning by shooting into the ceiling. Earp shortly appeared through a back door. He started toward Boyett, throwing open his coat and saying. "Boyett, I am unarmed; you have all the best of this," advancing as he spoke. Boyett warned him not to come nearer, but he did not heed the words, and when within eight feet Boyett fired, shooting him through the heart and killing him instantly.

Warren Earp was the youngest brother of the Earp family. He was well known by Under-Sheriff Paul of Tucson, who was Sheriff of Pima County in the eighties when trouble occurred between the Earps and the Clanton gang. Mr. Paul said this evening that the younger Earp came to this country about the time of the beginning of the feud from Colton, Cal. He was one of the original brothers and took an active part in their fights after he arrived.

Morgan Earp was killed in 1883 in Bob Hatch's saloon in Tombstone, being shot from the back as he was playing billiards. Virgil later was shot in the arm and seriously wounded in the killing of Frank Stilwell occurred in Tucson not long after, when he attempted to shoot Virgil through a car window. Stilwell was shot by Wyatt Earp.

Warren came here when his brothers got into trouble at Tombstone with the Clanton gang and he has remained here since. He was driving stage from Willcox to Fort Grant and had done freighting.

RECORD OF A FAMILY OF GUN FIGHTERS

Warren's Death Recalls the Great Battle with the

Clanton and McLowrie Gang in Tombstone.

The killing of Warren Earp at Willcox by Johnny Bogett closes the career on another of the Earp brothers whose names twenty years ago carried terror on the Arizona frontier.

A. H. Lewis, a Washington correspondent, formerly a newspaper reporter at Tombstone, A. T., gave the following interesting account of the notorious family, just after Wyatt Earp gave his decision against Fitzsimmons and his fight with Sharkey in San Francisco.

> In the early eighties, I was a neighbor of the Earp family. They abode at Tombstone, A. T., and did much toward making that hamlet a thrilling place of residence.
>
> Wyatt Earp is one of the five brothers who were abundant about Tombstone in 1881, 1882 and 1883. The community in 1883 assumed a positive attitude toward the Earps and presented a front to that household made up in the main of Winchesters and Colt six-shooters. The Earps construed this into lack of confidence on the part of the Tombstone public. They presented it by shaking the dust off Tombstone from their feet forever. They migrated to the Gunnison country. They were subsequently run out the Gunnison and Wyatt and Virgil Earp went to California, where Wyatt refereed the Fitzsimmons – Sharkey fight.
>
> The Earps were named respectively Virgil, Wyatt, Warren, Morgan, and Julian. They had a sister Jessie, who was with them in Tombstone. Of her as novelists say, more anon. Virgil was the oldest Earp, Wyatt the wisest, Morgan the most foolhardy, Julian the bravest and Jessie the most loving. As a result Wyatt and Virgil lived to get out of Tombstone and the Gunnison in advance of public opinion and the bullets that expressed it. While Morgan was killed in

Tombstone and Julian in Gunnison by Ike Clanton, who had married his sister Jessie and whom Wyatt and Virgil subsequently killed at Socorro – and Jessie, the loving one, wedded Ike Clanton, with whom the four brothers had a bloody feud at the time.

Wyatt Earp, and, for that matter, all the Earps, were gunfighters and men of prompt and bitter courage. Wyatt Earp himself is credited with ten men; one his own brother-in-law Clanton. Every one of the Earps had killed his men – not man – and were famed in Tombstone and in Cochise County round about as qualified to pull and make a center shot in less than one-tenth of a second. They had all filed the sights from their six-shooters when I knew them in '81 and '82; and, eschewing the intervention of a trigger, were prone to that prowess known as 'fanning their pistols' in a fight, whereby a Colts six-shooter becomes from the nonce a miniature Gatling.

In the early '80s, there were two factions in Tombstone. Virgil and Wyatt Earp led one– the stage robbers. Johnny Behan, Ike Clanton and Jack Ringo led the other – the rustlers. The stage robbers were in politics Republican, and stood up stages and plundered express companies for livelihood. The rustlers were Democrats, and devoted themselves to cattle stealing, murder, whiskey in the Faro bank as steady pursuits. In these days Johnny Behan was Sheriff of Cochise County and Virgil was a marshal of Tombstone. Behan, as stated belonged to the cow theft Democracy party, while Earp robbed stages and voted with the Republicans.

The Earps had treated themselves to many a killing. But there was no money and murder; nothing but relaxation. So they devoted themselves to holding up the stage. Virgil Earp had a combination with Barshel Williams, the Wells Fargo agent at Tombstone. When big money went out on the stage Williams tipped it off to Virgil Earp. The holdups were then planned in a convenient canyon. When the stake came along, at the words "Hands up!" Morgan Earp, who was a stage company guard, meekly put his arms over his head. Then the holdups went through the express pouches and boxes like the grace of heaven through a camp meeting.

There was never any shooting. It was from all standpoints a family affair, on the part of the Earps. Often they got as high as $25,000. After a robbery, the Earps made further money, enlisting themselves with a posse comitatus and chasing themselves. Virgil, as Marshal, would enlist Wyatt, Warren, Morgan and Julian, together with Curly Bill, their cousin, and hunt the hold-ups. It was a great industry, and by thus playing both ends against the middle, first robbing the stage and then pertaining to chase the robbers, the Earps waxed opulent.

But it came out on them. Williams, the Wells-Fargo agent, confessed. It happened thus: It was a gala occasion in the Bird Cage Opera-house, in Tombstone. Sheriff Johnny Behan, Ike Clanton, Ringo and others of the cow thieves had boxes on one side. The Earps, Curly Bill, Doc Holliday, Nixon and others of the stage robbers had boxes opposite. When one side cheered a performer the others hissed, and as the whiskey flew the spirits of both gangs mounted.

At last Ike Clanton took umbrage because Nixon opposite reposed his boot on the rail of his box. Ike Clanton was too far away for conversation, so in testimony of his condemnation of Nixon's action he pulled his gun and put a bullet through Nixon's offensive foot. It came off the box rail.

Much good and enthusiastic shooting ensued. Twelve men were killed and wounded. None of the Earps. Williams, the confederate of Virgil and Wyatt Earp, and the stage-robbing, was badly shot up. He expected to die and confessed. At this Wyatt and three of his brothers, with others of their gang, fortified themselves in an old adobe house on the edge of Tombstone. Behan and the cow thieves put in what time they could spare from the Faro bank and theft in besieging them. The siege was a stand-off. At last Morgan, the foolhardy one, heeled himself and came down from the adobe fortress to play Faro bank. He had just set a stack of blues on the king open when a cow thief listlessly put a bullet through his head.

Thus died the first of the Earps. There was more fighting then, and at last the Earps were driven out of Tombstone into the Gunnison. Their sister Jessie went with them. Ike Clanton, one of the Democrats and cow thieves followed them to Colorado and eloped with Jessie. This was too much for the Republican stage-robbing blood of Wyatt Earp and his brothers. They pursued. They ran Clanton and his bride into a mine tunnel. The miners interfered. There must be fair play. Ike Clanton offered to fight Virgil, Wyatt or Julian Earp for their sister. Julian took it up. The two shot it out with pistols and Julian was killed.

Thus died the second Earp. Ike Clanton and Jessie, now lived in peace two years then Wyatt Earp, Virgil Earp and Curly Bill crossed up with Clanton. And there was another feast of the guns. Clanton was killed and took with him Curly Bill to the happy hunting grounds. Wyatt Earp, when the smoke blew away, was also full of well-made bullet holes, but he got well.

It was then that Wyatt and Virgil Earp lined out for the slope. Just before they left Tombstone the Earps killed the two McLowries, Billy Clanton and Frank Stillwell. It was these killings, rather than the Wells-Fargo holdups, that caused the public to lay for them Wyatt Earp was prominent – with his gun – in the Cochise County seat war between Tombstone and Charleston of long ago.

His last public appearance in a gunplay was in the middle of the eighties, when Major Kelly ran Luke Short out of Dodge City, and the fugitive Luke summoned Wyatt Earp, Doc Holliday, Charlie Bassett, Bat Masterson and Shotgun Collins to aid him in the recovery of his own. They reinstated Luke and he and Kelly divided Dodge City between them.

The Earps Epilogue

The folklore surrounding the Earps will live for generations. The most famous brother Wyatt eventually made his way to California, before a brief stay in Alaska, then returning to California. His time in both states was not without controversy.

In 1896, he served as the referee in a San Francisco heavyweight boxing championship match between Tom Sharkey and Bob Fitzsimmons. The winner of the fight was to receive a prize of $10,000, which was a considerable amount at the time.

Fitzsimmons easily outfought Sharkey in the first seven rounds and was viewed as the inevitable winner. Then, in the eighth round, Fitzsimmons landed a smashing blow to Sharkey's abdomen, sending Sharkey to the mat withering in pain. The spectators jumped to their feet, celebrating Fitzsimmons's victory. But wait, here the story takes an unsavory turn.

Before the match, the two boxers and their managers could not agree upon a neutral referee. With just hours remaining before the match was to take place, Danny Lynch, Sharkey's manager, suggested his close friend Wyatt Earp oversee the match. The Fitzsimmons camp was highly suspicious of Wyatt's friendship with Lynch and, at first, objected. As time was running out, the Fitzsimmons camp finally agreed to Wyatt as the referee.

Back to the eighth round, as Sharkey withered on the canvas and Fitzsimmons joyously celebrated his victory in the ring, Danny Lynch jumped into the ring and quickly approached Wyatt. The two held a short, confidential conversation before Wyatt announced Sharkey as the winner. Fitzsimmons had not hit Sharkey in the abdomen, it was actually a low blow to the groin, and Wyatt disqualified Fitzsimmons.

The crowd unleashed its anger at Wyatt with vocalized "boos" and items thrown. They believed the fight was fixed. Soon rumors began circulating, which continued for months, that Wyatt had received $2,500 of the winnings purse to throw the fight to Sharkey.

In a subsequent court hearing, Wyatt denied fixing the fight and receiving the rumored $2,500. The judge dismissed the case since, at the time, boxing was illegal in San Francisco. As a result, Wyatt did not stand trial for throwing the fight, but he was convicted and fined $50.00 for bringing a .45 cal revolver, concealed under his coat, into the ring.

Wyatt was never able to distance himself from the alleged cheating scandal since a high percentage of people believed he did receive a payoff to throw the match. It followed him for the remainder of his life.

Following the boxing scandal, Wyatt made his way to Alaska. In 1900, Wyatt was reportedly shot while tending bar in an Alaska saloon. He survived and eventually returned to California.

Back in California, he served as a consultant for silent western movies where he became friends with western actors William Hart and Tom Mix. He also spent the fall, winter, and spring working his mining claims in the Southern California desert.

Interestingly, during his 1896 court testimony, Wyatt exposed the Long Green Examiner newspaper for writing fake news. In the article, the paper claimed it was based on an interview with Wyatt, but he swore under oath he never spoke with anyone from the Examiner.

In 1929, Wyatt, the last of the renowned brothers, died in Los Angeles.

THE DALTON GANG

AUTHOR'S COMMENTARY

For nearly two years, the Dalton Gang spread fear across the state of Oklahoma. They were an enterprising band of criminals focused on train and bank robberies, and other lesser crimes when presented with the opportunity. Ultimately, a botched double bank robbery brought a speedy end to the gang in a firestorm of bullets fired by the good citizens of Coffeyville, Kansas.

There was a distinct difference in the Dalton Gang compared to other marauding bands of criminals during the late 1890s; three of its members were brothers.

As the first story states, their exploits read like a dime novel.

The Star Gazette

Thursday, October 6, 1892

LIKE A DIME NOVEL.

The Infamous Dalton Gang Wiped

Out in Coffeyville, Kan.

ATTEMPTED TO ROB TWO BANKS.

In a Fight With a Marshal's Posse Four Outlaws Were Killed and One Fatally Wounded—A City Marshal and Three Citizens Also Dead.

COFFEYVILLE, Kas., Oct. 6.

The Dalton gang has been exterminated—wiped off the face of the earth. Caught like rats in a trap, they were yesterday shot down, but not until four citizens of this place had yielded up their lives in the work of extermination. Six of the gang rode into the town in the morning and robbed the two banks in the place. Their raid had become known to the officers of the law, and when the bandits attempted to escape they were attacked by the marshal's posse. In the battle which ensued four of the desperadoes were killed outright, and one was so badly wounded that he since has died. The other escaped, but is being hotly pursued. Of the attacking party four were killed, one fatally and two were severely injured.

The dead are: Bob Dalton, desperado, shot through the head; Grant Dalton, desperado, shot through the head; Emmett Dalton, desperado, shot through the left side; Joseph Evans, desperado, shot through the head; John Moore, "Texas Jack," desperado, shot through the head; T.C. Connelly, City Marshal, shot through the body; L.M. Baldwin, bank clerk, shot through the head; G.W. Cubine, merchant, shot through the head; C.J. Brown, shoemaker, shot through the body. Thomas G. Ayers, cashier for the First National Bank, was shot through the groin and cannot live. T.A. Reynolds of the attacking party has a wound in the right breast, but is not considered necessarily dangerous. Lais Detz, another of the attacking party, was shot in the right side. His wound is a serious one, but is not fatal.

It had been rumored a month ago that the Dalton gang was contemplating an immediate raid upon the banks of the city. Arrangements were made to give them a warm reception, and for over a week a patrol was maintained night and day to give warning of the gangs approach. The raid did not take place, and then came the report from Deming, N.M., that United States officers had had a battle with the band in that territory and three of the bandits had been killed. This report was believed here to have been circulated by the Daltons themselves, the intention being to divert attention from their real intentions, and to lull the people of the town into a sense of security. The people, however, were not so easily deceived, and when the report of the disaster to the gang in New Mexico was denied, vigilance was renewed. Still the expected raid was not made. Finally the patrol was withdrawn last Saturday, although every stranger was carefully scrutinized as soon as he appeared on the streets.

It was 9 o'clock in the morning when the Daltons rode into town. The came in two squads of three each, and passing through unfrequented streets, they rendezvoused in the alley in the rear of the First National Bank. They quickly tied their horses, and without losing a moment's time proceeded to the attack upon the banks.

Robert Dalton, the notorious leader of the gang, and Emmett, his brother, went to the First National Bank, the other four, under the leadership of "Texas Jack," or John Moore, going to the private bank of C.M. Congdon & Co.

The Dalton boys were born in this vicinity, and were well known to nearly every man, woman and child in town. In their progress through the town they had been recognized. City Marshal Connelly was quickly notified of their arrival, and almost before the bandits had entered the bank he was collecting a posse to capture them if possible, to kill them if necessary.

While the marshal was collecting his forces, the bandits, all ignorant of the trap that was being laid for them, were proceeding deliberately with their work of robbing banks. "Texas Jack's" band had entered Congdon's bank, and with their Winchesters leveled at Cashier Ball and Teller Carpenter, had ordered them to throw up their hands. Then Texas Jack searched them for weapons, while the other three desperados kept them covered with their rifles. Finding them to be unarmed, Cashier Ball was ordered to open the safe. The cashier explained that the safe's door was controlled by a time-lock, and that it could not by any means short of dynamite be opened before its time was up, which would be 10 o'clock, or in about twenty minutes.

"We'll wait," said the leader, and he sat down on the cashier's desk.

"How about the money drawers?" he suddenly asked, and, jumping up, he walked around to the cages of the paying and receiving tellers, and taking the money, amounting in all to less than $300, dumped in into a flour sack and again sat down.

Bob and Emmett Dalton in the meanwhile were having better luck at the First National Bank. When they entered the bank they found within Cashier Ayers, his son Albert Ayers, and Teller W.H. Shepperd. None of them were armed, and with leveled revolvers the brother bandits easily intimidated them. Albert Ayers and Teller Shepherd were kept under the muzzles of Emmett Dalton's revolvers, while Bob Dalton forced Cashier Ayers to strip the safe vault and cash drawers of all the money contained in them and place it in a sack.

Fearing to leave them behind lest they should give the alarm before the bandits should be able to mount their horses and escape, the desperadoes marched the officers of the bank out of the door, with the intention of keeping them under guard while they made their escape. The party made its appearance at the door of the bank just as Liveryman Spears and his companions of the marshal's posse took their positions in the square. When the Dalton brothers saw the armed men in the square, they appreciated their peril on the instant, and leaving the bank's officers on the steps of the bank building, ran for their horses. As soon as they reached the sidewalk Spear's rifle came quickly to position. An instant later it spoke, and Bob Dalton, the leader of the notorious gang, fell in his tracks dead. There was not a quiver of a muscle after he fell.

The bullet struck him in the right temple, and plowed through his brain, and passed out just above the left eye.

Emmett Dalton had the start of his brother, and before Spears could draw a bead on him he had dodged behind a corner of the bank.

The shot which dropped Bob Dalton aroused "Texas Jack's" band in Congdon's bank. Running to the windows they saw their leader prostrate on the ground. Raising their rifles to their shoulders, they fired one volley out of the windows. Two men fell at the volley. Cashier Ayers fell on the steps of the bank, shot through the groin. Shoemaker Brown of the attacking party in the square was shot through the body. He was quickly removed to his shop, but died just as he was carried within.

The firing attracted the attention of Marshal Connelly, who, collecting more men, ran hurriedly to the scene of the conflict.

After firing their volley from the window of the bank, the bandits, appreciating that their only safety lay in flight, attempted to escape. They ran from the door of the bank, firing as they fled. The Marshal's posse fired at the fleeing bandits. Spear's trusty Winchester spoke twice more in quick succession, and Joseph Evans and "Texas Jack" fell dead, both shot through the head. In the general fusillade, Grant Dalton, one of the two surviving members of Texas Jack's squad, Marshal Connelly, George Cubin, and L.M. Baldwin were mortally wounded and died in the field. Allie Ogee, the only survivor of the band, succeeded in escaping to the alley where the horses were tied, and mounting the swiftest horse of the lot, fled south in the direction of Indian Territory.

Emmett Dalton had already reached the valley in safety, but he had some trouble in getting mounted, and Allie

Ogee had already made his escape before Emmett got fairly started. Several of the posse, anticipating that horses would be required, were already mounted and pursued the fleeing bandits. Emmett Dalton's horse was no match for the fresher animals and his pursuers. As his pursuers closed on him he turned suddenly in his saddle and fired upon his would-be captors. The latter answered with a volley, and Emmett toppled from his horse, hard hit. He was brought back to town and died late in the afternoon. He made an antemortem statement, confessing to the various crimes committed by the gang of which he was a member. Allie Ogee had about ten minutes start of his pursuers, and was mounted on a swift horse. After the battle was over search was made for the money which the bandits had secured from the two banks. One sack was found under the body of Bob Dalton, and the other was found tightly clenched in Texas Jack's hand.

The bodies of those of the attacking party who were killed were removed to their respective homes, while the bodies of the bandits were allowed to remain where they had fallen until the arrival of the coroner from Independence, who ordered them removed to the courthouse. There he held an inquest, the jury returning a verdict in accordance with the facts. The inquest over the bodies of the citizens will be postponed until the result of the pursuit of Allie Ogee is known. During the time the bodies remained in the square they were viewed by hundreds of the people of this and surrounding towns, who having heard of the tragedy came in swarms to inspect the scene. The excitement was intense, and the fate of Ogee, should he be captured, will be hanging by the people.

EMMETT DALTON NOT DEAD

But He Cannot Live—His Confession—What He Says of Yesterday's Robbery.

COFFEYVILLE, Kan., Oct. 6

The report that Emmett Dalton had died from the effects of his wound was incorrect. He is still alive and is being closely guarded by a company of citizens under command of a deputy marshal. Only the newspaper correspondents are admitted to see him.

He confessed that the gang was responsible for the Red Rock, Wharton and other train robberies in the territory which had been credited to them. The story of hiding treasure, he said, was nonsense. "If there had been a hidden treasure," he declared, "We would have all been alive today. It was because we were all broke that we planned the Coffeyville raid. We were being hard pressed by the officers down in the territory, and Bob decided we would have to get out of the country. He planned the robbery about two weeks ago, while we were camped in the Osage country. He said he would outdo the James boys' exploits and would go to Coffeyville and raid both banks at the same time. We tried to dissuade him from it and then he called us cowards. That settled it and we started for the scene of the raid. We met at Tulas, and proceeded by easy stages to Timber Hill, twelve miles south of here, where we stopped Tuesday night. We started for Coffeyville at 6:30 yesterday morning and reached there at 9:30. You know the rest."

It was with great difficulty the bandit told his story, as he was suffering terribly from the wound in his side. The physician attending him says he can't possibly survive. Cashier Ayers is resting easier today, but his condition is critical. Nothing has been heard of the party in pursuit of Ogee. Rewards of $15,000 for the capture of the Daltons *or the delivery of their bodies to officers of the law are standing in the ticket office.*

ALLIE OGEE CONTINUED

The Cedar Valley Star

October 14, 1892

ALLIE OGEE

Can Easily Prove an Alibi

ALLIE OGEE IN WICHITA

WICHITA, Oct. 7.

Allie Ogee, who is thought to be the escaped member of the Dalton gang, and whom the Coffeyville posse is pursuing, as it supposes in the territory, is in this city, and has been here continually for the past nine months working in the Dold Packing house. He can prove by hundreds of friends that he was not out of the city during the past month. The posse is evidently after the wrong man.

Dr. Wood, of Coffeyville, Ogee's foster-father, is here today, and says he cannot understand how Ogee's name became connected with that of the Daltons'. As boys they knew one another, but Ogee always disliked the Daltons, and they had never been together of recent years. Dick Broadwell, of Hutchinson, "Texas Jack's" brother, passed through here last night for Coffeyville to see if it was really his brother who was killed. He says that he did not know that his brother was connected with the Dalton gang.

The North Adams Transcript

Monday, June 22, 1896

DYNAMITE DICK

(Special Dispatch to the Transcript.)

GUTHRIE, Okla., June 22

Dynamite Dick, alias Dan Wiley, the last member of the Dalton gang, was captured yesterday and charged with the murder of four deputy marshals.

The Oklahoma Leader

Thursday, December 10, 1896

DYNAMITE DICK IS DEAD

Jealous Deputy Marshals Working the Black Craig Fake

It seems that Dynamite Dick is dead after all and that the "Black Craig" story was a fake sprung by certain envious deputies. The Leader gets the following interesting particulars from Blackwell: "Dynamite Dick," the outlaw who was killed near here last Friday morning, was thoroughly identified by several persons who have known him for years. There is no longer any doubt about the dead man being the notorious outlaw Dynamite Dick, although there is an effort being made by the deputy United States marshals to create the false idea that it is some other person.

The cause of the deputy marshals acting thus is simply jealousy, owing to the fact that they had no hand in the fight, and are chagrined over the fact that Zip Wyatt and "Dynamite Dick," two of the most desperate outlaws ever known to exist in the territory successfully evaded the deputy United States marshals, but finally met death at the hands of unassuming farmers.

As there is an aggregated reward of nearly $4,000 upon "Dynamite Dick," he was a valuable prize to Marshal Nagle's force, and the loss of this is very humiliating to say the least.

The Paola Times Kansas

Thursday, 4 May, 1899

Dalton Wants a Pardon

TOPEKA, Kan., May 4

Emmett Dalton, the surviving member of the Dalton gang, who is now serving a life sentence in the Kansas penitentiary for assisting in the famous Coffeyville raid in 1891, has applied to Governor Stanley for a pardon.

AUTHOR'S COMMENTARY

In July 1937, Emmett Dalton, the last survivor of the Dalton gang, died in his Los Angeles home at the age of sixty-six. Newspaper reports allege during his outlaw days he managed to survive being shot twenty-three times. Emmett received a life sentence for bank robbery and was released and pardoned after serving fourteen and a half years. He moved to Los Angeles around 1920, joined a church, and campaigned for prison reform. He dabbled in real estate, wrote the book, When the Daltons Rode, and worked in the film industry as a scenario writer and background actor.

BIGFOOT
THE RENEGADE
AUTHOR'S COMMENTARY

We have all heard stories of Bigfoot, the massive hairy beast inhabiting the remote wilderness and striking fear into those it encounters. In this case, Bigfoot was genuine. He was considered a giant of a man during his time and also by today's standards; standing six feet eight inches and weighing in at three hundred pounds, he was a terrifying force.

He was a consummate warrior and killer. His name struck fear into all. I reviewed several stories covering Bigfoot's adventures, and they all reveal the markers of truth. Today, he is unknown to the vast majority of Americans, but now his legend will live.

Twin Falls Weekly News

Friday, January 26, 1906

BIGFOOT

The Gigantic and Bloodthirsty Renegade

Who Led the Piute Band of the Snake Indians in Their Raids Upon

Emigrant Trains Along Snake River in the Early Days.

Story of His Misdeeds

Related by Himself After He Had Been Mortally

Wounded by J.W. Wheeler in a Sensational Duel on Reynolds Creek.

CLOSE to the old emigrant road, near the point where it crosses Cedar draw, about 10 miles west of Twin Falls, are four mounds. They mark the resting place of four men who fell in combat with the Indians many years ago. The graves are easily discernible but they might be mistaken for badger mounds. The grave of another Indian victim is located near the top of the grade at Clark's Ferry, and there are two more at Lewis Ferry, all on the Twin Falls tract.

Now that the tract is being settled up, and by people who are unfamiliar with the early history of Idaho, there is danger of the graves being plowed over. Efforts are being made to locate all of the graves and, if possible, have them fenced in and marked. The identity of the victims will be established, if it is possible to do so. It is not believed that any farmer will begrudge a few feet of ground to be consecrated to the memory of those who blazed the trail to the West before days of steel rails and Pullman cars.

In the early days many bands of bloodthirsty savages roamed the Snake River valley. The stretch of country between the Goose Creek mountains and the Salmon river in Cassia county was infested with Indians. The sagebrush plain afforded little cover and many and bloody were the fights that took place. Whole trains of emigrants, composed of men, women and children, were slaughtered without mercy, the bones of many being left to bleach on the banks of the Snake and Boise rivers, testifying to the deadly hatred of the Snake Indians to the whites. In some cases the emigrants were able to bury their dead, in other instances they had to flee for their lives and leave the bodies to the coyotes.

The leader and the most desperate of all the Indians between Oregon and Utah during the '60's was one known as Bigfoot, who, like the gigantic monster, as he truly was, roamed over the plains and mountains of Idaho with a small band of picked warriors, committing murders and depredations. They range from the Grand Ronde valley in eastern Oregon to the heads of the Owyhee and Weiser rivers and along the Snake river valley in Idaho.

Many stories were told of the great size of this noted Indian desperado and about the size of his feet. Whenever a depredation was committed those large moccasin tracks were certain to be found among others. While the other Indians were sometimes mounted on ponies he was always on foot. One reason for this, perhaps, was that no ordinary horse could carry him, and the following account will show that he had but little use for a horse, for the rapidity with which he traveled from place to place was the wonder and surprise of the settlers on the Snake and Boise rivers. One day his fresh tracks would be seen on the Weiser and the next day he would be heard of on the Owyhee, 75 or 80 miles distant.

One day he was chased by J. W. Wheeler, Frank Johnson and a man of the name of Cook, who are all well mounted, while Bigfoot, as usual, was traveling on foot with two other Indians. Wheeler and his two companions were camped near the head of the Malheur river. In the night their horses gave indications that Indians were prowling near the camp, so a close watch was kept until daylight, when, on examination of the ground, it was discovered that old Bigfoot and two other Indians had been within a few yards of the camp during the night. Upon making this discovery the three white men became excited and eager for the chase.

Bigfoot had been treading on dangerous ground. Here were three as cool and determined men as ever put foot out west, all of them crack marksman, well accustomed to Indian fighting and three better horsemen could not have been found in the territory.

After a hasty breakfast, all mounted their horses and took the trail, Frank Johnson remarking, "Well, boys, we will make it hot for old Bigfoot today."

Wheeler replied laughingly, "Yes, and it will make it hot for our horses to catch up with that old leather-headed devil if he can travel as far in a day as Enoch Fruit says he can." Enoch Fruit was a noted horse thief, who once kept ferry at Farewell Bend on the Snake river, and he had often met Bigfoot and often talked with him. It was through Fruit that the fact was first known that Bigfoot could speak English and that it came to be believed that the big-footed fiend belonged to some other tribe of Indians than the one he was with, which in time proved to be true.

Chase Through the Brush.

The three men rode in hot pursuit. A fierce ride for two hours brought them in sight of the Indians, who are going on a rapid trot towards the Snake river. All hands are now prepared in earnest for the chase. The big Spanish Spurs were applied without mercy to the already bleeding flanks of their faithful and spirited horses.

The two smaller Indians were soon overtaken and shot down. They made a determined and desperate resistance but their horses and arrows and old-style guns proved of no avail before the Henry rifle in the hands of the men they now had to deal with. By the time these two Indians were dispatched, old Bigfoot was at least a mile ahead, running and jumping the sagebrush like a deer, increasing the distance between him and his pursuers where the ground was roughest and losing where the ground was better.

The exciting chase was kept up in this way for over 30 miles with about the same result, until at last the huge monster reached the Snake river and, plunging into the stream, struck out swimming for the opposite shore. He proved himself to be an excellent swimmer, as well as a skillful runner, carrying his gun and ammunition above water. The faithful horses we now put down to their best speed but only reached the bank in time for their riders to see, much to their disappointment and disgust, the tall form of Bigfoot clambering out of the water on the other bank.

Johnson shouted out: "Boys, look there; don't Bigfoot beat hell?"

Cook said, "Yes, and he beat our horses, too."

Wheeler quietly remarked that if old Bigfoot did not have the rheumatism after running so far and then swimming that cold water, he deserved to be remembered as a living specimen of health and endurance.

In the meantime, Bigfoot, having gained the bank of the river and shaken himself, gave an unearthly yell and shouted in plain English, "Come over, come over, you damned cowards," and then dived into the willows. The poor bleeding and foaming horses were completely fagged out and so were their riders. Many times during the day the horses had plunged into badger holes, falling and pitching their reckless riders over their heads.

Bigfoot Escapes.

The next move was to go some five miles down the river and cross at the nearest ferry, which was then kept by Mr. Packwood, and then come up the river and try to strike the trail of the Indian again. This the white men did, following his enormous tracks for a few miles to the mouth of Weiser river. Here they found that the object of their pursuit had caught two of the largest size salmon, roasted them and eaten every morsel, leaving the bones picked clean. He had then taken the back track along the Snake river and swam back to the side from which he had been chased.

Night came and found three of the angriest and hungriest men who had ever lain down on the banks of the Snake River. Instead of growling over their disappointment, as most men would have done, they spent the evening in joking and recounting the many incidents of the day. It was agreed by all that old Bigfoot could outrun and out-wind any Indian on the record, and that he was the largest man and had the largest foot by half of any man they had ever seen; also that he was a dear lover of fish, as evidenced by the skeletons he had left at his last campfire.

Next morning the chase was for the time abandoned, Wheeler remarking that he would get even on that "old son of a cricket eater" if it took him five years for having caused him to ruin his fine horse and almost break his own neck. The resolve was realized, but not until nearly two years afterwards, during which time Bigfoot sent many a poor, unfortunate miner and teamster to that land from whence no traveler returns.

Took Many Scalps.

Bigfoot's favorite field of slaughter was between Boise and Silver City, where the road passed through a narrow defile between table rocks or bluffs, a few miles south of Snake river. It was among these bluffs that this noted chief and his braves lurked and picked off many of Idaho's first settlers. Scarcely a week passed that someone was not killed, while traveling to or from the Owyhee country.

It was near this place that Bigfoot afterwards met his death in a way he least expected, just in sight of the spot where he had murdered Ulman Lamot, a man of the name of Baker and a partner of Charles Adams. He had also shot Charles Adams through the hand and had killed a score of others whose names are not recalled. The last man known to have been killed by Bigfoot and his little band was a Mr. Jarvis, who was on his way from Boise to Owyhee with a load of eggs and vegetables. A Chinaman, who was riding with Jarvis, was killed at the same time. This occurred in 1868, just before Bigfoot himself was sent to the happy hunting grounds by Wheeler.

This narrative was related by William T. Anderson, a former resident of Idaho, who afterwards moved to California. To those who were familiar with conditions in the territory at that time, Anderson's story bore every mark of truthfulness. His description of the death of Bigfoot was graphic and veracious. In 1878 he gave the following account of the incident to the Boise Statesman:

Bigfoot's Last Fight.

As I am perhaps the only white man now living – unless Wheeler is yet alive – who knows how or when this noted chief Bigfoot met his death, I will give as true and faithful an account of the thrilling and deadly encounter as possible, and the reasons why it was kept from the world so long.

In the spring of 1868 I was working at the carpenter's trade in Silver City, Idaho. It was at the time of the great lawsuit and the pitched battle which was fought over the Golden Chariot quartz lode, in which many lives were lost on both sides and which resulted in the death of the two owners of the disputed ground, namely, Marion More and Samuel Lockhart. The whole town was in an uproar and a terrible state of excitement existed. Everybody went armed to the teeth. Governor Ballard resolved to place the town under martial law and many came over from Boise City to assist in the somewhat dangerous undertaking. Among those who came I noticed a tall, fine-looking young man of rather slight but handsome build, with small hands and feet. He had dark brown hair and a smooth face with dark, steel-gray eyes, expressive of intelligence and a kind heart. Though there was something striking in the appearance of the man, little did I think he could look death in the face with a smile, or without the slightest change of countenance, but such was the character of the man I was made acquainted with Wheeler by Captain Hatch, who is also a carpenter and a refined gentleman.

He knew Wheeler well, having been on a prospecting tour with him, and had also mined near him or with him at one time. Wheeler was a good-hearted fellow and was the life of the camp and of every circle into which he came, but he was at the same time one of the bravest and most determined men in the territory. He was as strong and active as a panther, and a better marksman than any man he ever met in his life. Though a peaceable and temperate man, the desperados all knew him and never offered to infringe upon his rights.

An Awkward Plight.

This was the last time I saw Wheeler until I met him on the scene where the terrible combat – Bigfoot's last fight –

took place. This happened in the latter part of July, 1868. I was going from Silver City to Boise, traveling alone with a two-horse wagon. When near the dangerous pass where so many had been killed, I, being unarmed, concluded to layover and let my horses graze until I should have company through the canyon, so I foolishly turned my horses loose and set myself to cooking something to eat. While thus engaged, my horses got frightened at something and ran away, leaving me afoot and alone and badly frightened. I followed the horses' tracks and found they had gone down Reynolds creek in the direction of the massacre ground. As the creek runs through this bluff of rocks within a half mile of where the road does, I followed them and found they had started through the canyon.

I had just turned back, afraid to go farther, when, to my horror and surprise, I looked across the creek and saw three Indians coming at full speed. They were painted and feathered, and as they were coming directly towards me, I felt certain that they saw me and I thought my time had come. The tall and terrible looking Indian, who could be none other than Bigfoot himself, was some 50 yards ahead of another Indian, while the third was an equal distance behind the second one. I stood paralyzed with fear. The only chance left me was to hide behind some rocks and there await my fate which, I felt certain, within a few minutes be death. So I crouched down behind a ledge of rocks and bid a last farewell to home and friends, as I then thought, expecting that in a few minutes my dripping scalp would be hanging to the belt of the most horrible looking monster I had ever beheld. It would be useless for me to attempt to describe my feelings at this moment. In less than a minute old Bigfoot came thundering along like an old buffalo bull, within less than 30 yards of me. He did not halt but made straight for the road, which was not far off. I looked *and saw the stage full of passengers, with several females among the number, just coming in sight.*

Close Call for the Stage.

Somewhat to my relief I now discovered that it was the stage and not myself that was the object of Bigfoot's attention. He had evidently resolved to head off the stage, murder the driver and rob the passengers. He was destined, however, to do no more scalping on this side of the 'dark river.'

When the Indian who was next to the chief was opposite my hiding place, my blood was chilled by the crack of a rifle which dropped this Indian dead within 20 yards of me. At the report of the gun old Bigfoot jumped behind a large rock and the hindmost Indian broke back over the hill and was not seen again. For a moment all was quiet. I saw Charley Barnes throw the silk gracefully over his horses, as was his habit on nearing the canyon; he and the passengers all unconscious of the terrible fate they had just escaped. I afterwards learned that among the passengers were Judge Roseborough, Charley Douglas, the gambler, and Mrs. Record and her daughter. Mr. Record and family were then keeping the stage station at the fifteen-mile house, between Boise City and the Snake river. Little did they think that there was one so near them as I was and in such a terrible plight, who dared not move or ask for aid, and that the most deadly and bloody encounter was about to take place that had been witnessed by any of us.

Indian Strategy Fails.

Those few minutes seemed like hours to me. I knew that an Indian had been killed near me, but by whom or from what direction I could form no idea. From Bigfoot's action it was evident that he thought the report of the gun came from a tree surrounded by a clump of willows near the creek, some 80 yards from where he stood. The sequel proved that he was right. A few minutes after the stage passed out of sight Bigfoot commenced practicing a bit of strategy that was new to me. All I could do was to lie still and in dead silence watch his movements. First he would crawl to one side of the large rock behind which he was hiding, then crawl back to the other side and cautiously peep around the side of the rock, but no one shot at him. All was dead quietude. He would then put his ear to the ground and listen but could not hear the slightest noise. At last he tried another plan of escape. He tied a large bunch of sagebrush to his back and started to crawl away. To my great horror he advanced directly toward the spot where I lay hidden behind the ledge of rocks. He came slowly and gently toward me. I was undecided to remain where I was or jump and run toward the clump of willows which Bigfoot had been watching so long and take chances of finding a white man. If I remained where I was much longer, Bigfoot, who had not yet seen me, could not fail to find me. But this terrible state of suspense was soon brought to an end.

Wheeler to the Rescue.

When Bigfoot had crawled over about half the distance that separated his hiding place from mine, I heard a clear voice ring out on the mountain air and cool, deliberate tones, saying: 'Get up from there, Bigfoot, you old featherheaded, leather-bellied coward. I can see you crawling off like a snake. This is one time that you did not even get a woman's scalp. Here's a scalp. Come down to take mine, you coward.'

At this Bigfoot sprang to his feet and leveled a large double-barrel rifle at the willows and said: 'You coward; me no coward. You come out; I'll scalp you too.'

At this Wheeler sprang out from among the bushes in plain view, saying: 'Here I am; now sail in, old rooster.'

Both men fired almost at the same instant. Bigfoot staggered but recovered and fired again, then threw his gun down and started to run toward the dead Indian. He ran but a few yards when another shot caused him to reel again but he succeeded in reaching the spot where the dead Indian lay and, picking up the gun left by the latter where he had fallen, he leveled it toward Wheeler and fired again, just at the moment that Wheeler's gun sent another unerring bullet into his powerful frame. Bigfoot again staggered and came very near falling, but again recovered and, drawing a knife, gave an unearthly whoop which almost froze my blood and then started toward Wheeler.

He had gone but a few yards when another shot staggered him and another. I was dumb with fear, apprehending that after all the Indian might succeed in reaching Wheeler and then grasp him in his powerful clutches. Wheeler never moved from the spot where he stood, but, handling his gun with extraordinary skill, continued to fire until at last, when within 30 yards of him, the huge red demon fell with a broken leg to rise no more. Wheeler, however, emptied the balance of the 16 shots into him and then, without moving out of his tracks, reloaded his rifle and said: 'How do you like the way my gun shoots, old hoss?' I bet my scalp against yours that you don't scalp anymore white men in this canyon very soon.'

Bigfoot cried out in plain English, 'Don't shoot me anymore, you have killed me.'

Wheeler walked up near the Indian and, pulling out an ivory-handled revolver, gazed a moment at his fallen foe, then shouted to me, 'Come down, whoever you are, there is no danger now.'

I went to the spot and found Bigfoot bleeding from 12 wounds, both legs and one arm broken. The Indian asked for water, when Wheeler said: 'Hold on until I break that other arm, then I'll give you a drink.'

Bigfoot said: 'Well, do it quick and give me a drink and let me die.'

Wheeler leveled his pistol and at the report the arm fell useless to the ground. This to some may seem cruel but I was yet afraid to go near this powerful and desperate savage monster. Wheeler went down to the creek and brought up his canteen full of water and placed it to the mouth of the Indian, who drank it all. Bigfoot then said he wished he had some whiskey, when Wheeler said he had a small bottle of whiskey and ammonia which he always carried in case of snake bites; that Bigfoot could have that if he thought it would do him any good.

Bigfoot said: 'Give it to me quick, I'm getting blind.'

Wheeler gave him a pint flask filled with the strong liquid, mixed with a little water. The Indian drank it, every drop, and then said: 'I'm sick and blind,' and then fell back, apparently dead.

Wanted His Scalp Saved.

After a few minutes he revived and said he was better. He asked us to wash the dust and paint from his face and see what a good-looking man he was. We complied with his request and, to our surprise, we found a fine-looking face with the handsomest set of teeth we ever beheld. He had large, black but wicked looking eyes. His complexion had been almost white but was now, of course, badly tanned. He had a heavy shock of long, black hair, somewhat inclined to be kinky. He was of enormous size and such hands, especially feet, I never saw on any mortal before or since. He soon began to be quite talkative and expressed a wish that we would make him one promise. Wheeler asked him what it was. He asked that we should not scalp him nor take him to Boise City after he died, but to drag him among the willows, pile rocks upon him and lay his old gun by his side.

'If you will promise me this,' he said, 'I will die satisfied.' Wheeler told him that if he would tell him who he was and where he came from he would perhaps promise and do what he wished but that he must answer all the questions he was asked and tell the truth.

Tempting Reward.

Bigfoot then said: 'I have been a very bad man and if I tell you all that I have done I'm afraid you will not do what I have asked of you.'

Wheeler said: 'I know you have been a bad man but if you will tell me everything I will not tell anyone that you are dead nor tell anyone about you.' When Wheeler said this Bigfoot seemed to brighten up and said: 'Now, do keep your promise and I will tell you my whole history and all that I have gone through if I can only live long enough to do so.'

Wheeler said: 'I have been assured by prominent citizens of Boise City that if anyone killed you and brought your scalp and your feet to Fort Boise, at least $1000 would be paid for them, for you have done a great deal of mischief, killed a great many white people, and everybody thinks you were one of the party that killed Mrs. Scott and her husband on Burnt river last fall, as your big tracks are found the next day near the scene of the murder, as they have always been found when white people have been killed by Indians in this part of the country. I have now been out here four days, waiting for you, and the mosquitoes have nearly eaten me up while hiding in the willows, but now, if it will do you any good, I will hide you, but I will break your gun so that other Indians will not use it again.'

Bigfoot's Bloody Story.

The following is Bigfoot's account of himself and his career, taking down just as it was related to Wheeler and myself:

'I was born in the Cherokee nation. My father was a white man named Archer Wilkinson. He was hanged for murder in the Cherokee nation when I was a small boy. My mother was part Cherokee and part negro, so I was told. She was a good Christian woman. My name is Starr Wilkinson. I was thus named after Thomas Starr, a noted desperado in the nation. I was always called Bigfoot Wilkinson as long as I can remember. The boys always made fun of me when I was a boy, because I was so large for my age and had such big feet. I had a bad temper and got to drinking when quite young and got to be so strong that when anyone would call me a nickname I would fight him. In this way I came near killing several with my fist. I found that I would soon be killed if I remain in the country, so I ran away from home and went to Tiloqua, then the capital of the Cherokee nation. There I fell in with some emigrants who were going to Oregon in 1856 and I drove a team across the plains for my board. The folks I traveled with were very kind to me. I fell in love with a young lady of the company who thought a good deal of me until we fell in with the company from New York.

Along with these new people was an artist who was a smart, good looking fellow. He soon cut me out. After this the young lady would hardly notice me or speak to me. I knew then that he had told her something bad about me.

'He made fun of me several times and, while we were camped near the Goose creek mountains (in the vicinity of the present site of Burley) he and I went out one morning to hunt up the stock. We went to the bank of the Snake river. I asked him what he intended to do when he got to Oregon

and he said he was going to marry and settle down. I told him he should not do so for I thought I had the best right to her. He only laughed and said: "Do you suppose she would marry a big-footed nigger like you and throw off on a good-looking fellow like me?" This made me mad and I told him I was no negro and that if he called me that again I would kill him.

'So he drew his gun on me and repeated it again. I was unarmed but started at him. He shot me in the side but did not hurt me much, so I grabbed him and threw him down and choked him to death, then threw him into the Snake River, took his gun, pistol and knife and ran off into the hills.

Joined the Indians.

The emigrants did not leave camp for a few days. They were, perhaps, hunting for us. Some of them went on to Oregon but the family that I had been traveling with went back with some others to Salt Lake, where they wintered. I made my way to the Boise river, where I found a French trader and trapper and a man named Joe Lewis. This Joe Lewis was one who helped to massacre Dr. Whitman and many others near old Fort Walla Walla in 1847. He was a bad man, but he was a good friend to me when I needed a friend. So I went with him and joined the Indians and have been with them ever since. In 1857 I went with Lewis and some Indians near the emigrant road for the purpose of stealing stock from the emigrants. In one of our raids I found cattle that I knew had belonged to the family I had crossed the plains with the year before. So I determined to go to the train and see if my girl was with them and try to get her to run off with me. I found her but she was very mad with me, as were all the rest. They said they thought I had killed Mr. Hart, the artist, and that I ought to hang for it. They told me to leave the camp. I told the girl that if she did not have me she would be sorry for it before she reached Oregon.

I had to leave but was determined to have revenge, so I took Joe Lewis and 30 Indians and followed down the Boise river where it empties into the Snake river and massacred them and ran off all their stock and killed the girl too. I am sorry for that now, for she was a good girl, but it was too late to be sorry now. I was mad and foolish. I have been in several other massacres. I helped to kill the Scott family on Burnt river. We wanted their horses. I also helped to kill an officer and took his wife prisoner last fall. The officer was on his way to Camp Lyon. His wife got sick, had a child and could not ride, so some of the Indians killed her. I had a squaw for a wife and when Jeff Stanford was out with a lot of men fighting us they killed my wife and carried off my little boy. Since that time I have done all the mischief I could and I am glad of it.

Fate of Joe Lewis.

Wheeler here asked Bigfoot what became of Joe Lewis. He said Joe Lewis was shot by a man who carried the express from Auburn to Boise in 1862. While Lewis was trying to steal some horses on the Payette river one night, the expressman shot across the river with buckshot, hitting Lewis in the side and wounding Bigfoot in the leg. As it was getting dark and neither of the wounded men spoke, the expressman did not know that anyone had been hit. 'Joe whispered to me,' continued Bigfoot, 'that he was hurt bad, so I took him up on my back and started to run with him but he soon died and I covered him up in the sand on the bank of the Payette river where he was never found by the whites. That was the last of poor Joe, and I hope you will do that much for me.'

Mr. Wheeler said: 'All right, Mr. Wilkinson, I guess I will do it, as I am from the Cherokee nation myself and have a little Cherokee blood in my veins, I will not refuse to grant your dying request.'

When Wheeler said this and assured him that he would not take his body, or any portion of it, to the Fort, Bigfoot actually wept and asked to know Wheeler's name and said: 'You are a brave man and I know you will keep your word. I am a brave man, too, but you shot a little too quick for me and you had the best gun and you have killed me. Your shot struck me just as I was pulling the trigger, else I think I should have killed you as I hardly ever missed anything I ever shot at. I got my old gun at the massacre in 1857. I do not know how many men I have killed with it.'

Medicine Man's Dream.

Bigfoot then continued: 'Nearly all of our little band of warriors are killed off. There are but five left who have been running with me. You have just killed one of the bravest of the band. He has been one of my head braves ever since the Indians recognized me as the leader of the brave little band. His father is an old medicine man and he told us when we left not to go on this trip for he had dreamed about us. He dreamed that there was a large snake secreted in these bluffs that had a white man's head on it, and had a medicine gun, that when he pointed it at the Indians, they could not see how to shoot and that after killing them he broke their guns to pieces.

He wept when we left camp and said he should never see us again until we met in spirit land. He was right. If I had minded him we would not have been killed.'

Wheeler said: 'Well, if you meet the old medicine gentleman in spirit land, tell him he was a good hand at dreaming if he did call me a snake.'

Wheeler then asked him where the rest of the Indians were camped. Bigfoot said: 'This is something I cannot tell, but I will tell you anything else you may ask me. There are but few of them left, and now that we are killed the rest will soon go into the Fort and it would do you no good to kill them.

'The little band I run with call themselves Piutes; the rest call themselves Fish Indians, because they live by fishing on the Malheur and Snake rivers and do not run with the Lake Piutes and the Bannocks. The other Indians are not friendly toward us and I care nothing about them; but our little band had been brave Indians. They have always treated me well and I do not wish to betray them as the last act of a bad life.'

Wheeler said: 'Bully for you, Wilkinson; I think more of you than I did before, for you are not a traitor if you have been a bad man otherwise.' Wheeler asked him how tall he was and how much he weighed. Bigfoot said he did not know, for he had grown very much since he joined the Indians; that when he left the whites he was about 19 years old; that he then measured six feet six inches and a half in height and weighed 255 pounds. 'But I know,' he said, 'that I must weigh at least 300 pounds and there is not a pound of fat on me,' which was true. His voice had failed. He fell back, saying, 'Everything is getting dark,' and then lay silent for a while. Then he spoke in husky, rapid tones, 'Look, look, the soldiers are after me. I must go, quick, quick.' Then he died without a struggle.

A Physical Giant.

Bigfoot was a model of strength and endurance. I had a tape line and rule in my pocket with which I took the following exact measurements of this wonderful being. Around the chest he measured 59 inches, height six feet eight and one-

half inches, length of foot 17 ½ inches, around the ball of the foot 18 inches, around the widest part of the hand 18 inches. I am confident that he must have weighed at least 300 pounds, and all bone and sinew, not a pound of surplus flesh on him.

We then got my horses, put a rope around Bigfoot's body, to which we hitched the horses and dragged the body some 150 yards to the creek. We threw some brush and rocks upon him, hid the other broken gun and left the other Indian where he had fallen. Wheeler said the other Indians would probably come and burn what was left if they were not afraid.

We then started for Boise City, when we arrived the next day. Wheeler made me promise to say nothing about the affair, as he had given his word to Bigfoot and was resolved not to break the promise he had made.

THE BLACK HAND & THE MAFIA

AUTHOR'S COMMENTARY

No one can pinpoint the precise year the first group of the Black Hand (Mano Nera) began criminal activities in New York. It appears they started in the early 1890s and remained in operation until 1920 when the more familiarly known Mafia took over. The Black Hand was comprised only of Sicilian immigrants. They focused on the Italian communities by targeting individuals they believed were wealthy.

Their main areas of focus were extortion, kidnappings, bombings, and murder. In most cases, the blackmail demand was delivered by letter. It stated the amount of cash demanded, when and where it must be delivered, and the consequences of disobeying their demands. Scores of businesses and tenement houses were bombed when their demands were refused, and dozens of people were gunned down.

In the beginning, the Black Hand kept their criminal activities confined to the Italian immigrant community. They were familiar with the language and customs and were, therefore, easily able to identify targets for their criminal plots. As time passed and they became familiar with the English language and customs, they realized there were wealthy members of other ethnic groups. If they believed you had some money, you became a target. They immediately expanded their criminal ventures to include all ethnic groups in New York and increased their operations to Chicago, New Orleans, Kansas City, and other American cities.

As a former detective, I investigated traditional Mafia organized crime families during the 1970s and early 1980s; it is clear the Black Hand was considerably more violent than their latter brethren. Granted, the Mafia I dealt with were violent but rarely engaged in the indiscriminate use of explosives or kidnapping.

I have included two of the hundreds of available articles which provide an excellent window into the nature of the criminal activities of the Black Hand.

The Washington Post

Sunday, April 21, 1907

GRIM RECORD OF BLACK HAND TERRIFIES CHICAGO.

From the Chicago Record-Herald.

Over the homes of many Italians and other residents of Chicago a grim shadow lowers. It is the shadow of a Black Hand grasping either a poniard or a revolver. Behind the spectral, minatory figure lurks an organization – secret, soulless, banded together for the purpose of plunder or revenge, principally plunder. This sometimes is affected in the form of violent robbery, but more frequently by the means of dire threats for blackmailing purposes.

This desperate organization is no respecter of persons, and apparently knows no nationality in the scope of its lawless work. A distinctively of Italian inception, it preys most often on compatriots from the sunny realm of Victor Emmanuel III. A few recent cases will afford positive proof of this assertion.

Revenge with Dynamite.

Early last Sunday morning, residents in the vicinity of the East Chicago Avenue Police Station were aroused by a *terrific explosion. Because he refused to give up $500 an effort was made to destroy Giuseppe Mancusco and family, living at 92 Milton avenue. Two sticks of dynamite were used. One was placed in the rear of the house, and when exploded almost wrecked the back part of the structure. When policeman Sanders ran to the house, he found a burning fuse under the front steps of the dwelling. It was attached to a long stick of dynamite, enough to have blown the house into fragments.*

Mancusco has been a quiet resident of the neighborhood for twenty years. He has accumulated a moderate competency in the grocery business. He has no enemies, but apparently the Black Hand is determined to wrest from him part of his savings. For two months he has been receiving threatening letters from the "Six Friends" branch of the Black Hand, demanding that he make payment. Mancusco took the letters to the police. He was instructed to prepare a decoy package of money and leave it at the appointed place. The police secreted themselves for several nights, hoping to catch the blackmailers. But their efforts were unavailing.

Mancusco was promptly notified that the Black Hand was aware that he had reported the matter to the police, and that his life would now pay the penalty. The attempt to destroy his dwelling was the result.

Mystery in a Murder.

Grazio Dato, thirty-four years of age, arrived in Chicago six weeks ago from England. He went straight to the Southwest side, where he met some of his countrymen. Evidently, he had known one or two of them in Italy. He associated and drank with them.

Suddenly one morning was heard the sound of a pistol shot in front of 96 Law avenue, where Grazio had been stopping. Voices of men quarreling had been heard by the boarding-house keeper. The police came and found Dato dead with a bullet hole in his head.

A dozen Italians were arrested, but the police learned nothing. What was it? Had Dato incurred enmity or vengeance of some secret society? Why was he killed so quickly after reaching this country? Had he been followed by spies? Was he a member of the Mafia, was he an anarchist, or was he simply a Black Hand victim? The police, if they have any theory at all, think the last named the most likely.

A man, supposed to be Carmen Chappelo, arrived in Chicago three months ago from Italy. He knew no one in America – at least he was not supposed to have enemies here. His terribly mangled body was found at 101st and the Illinois Central tracks chopped into bits by a train, yet the portions of the body picked up bore cut and stab wounds which show plainly that Chappelo had been murdered before his body was placed on the tracks. Why was Chappelo killed? It is not known that he had money. Did he fall victim to some secret society mandate? The police don't know and have given up trying to find out.

Dread of the Black Hand.

The Black Hand. What is it? Whence did it come? There is no definite answer to the questions. But that the Black Hand, a secret Italian murder and blackmail organization does exist in the United States has been proven without a doubt.

There have been perhaps 100 cases of Black Hand outrages reported in Chicago. Police think that there have been hundreds of other cases that never have been reported, the victims preferring silence to the fear of punishment at the hands of the secret assassins.

The Chicago experiences do not widely differ from the happenings in other parts of the country. One day we have a store blown to splinters in the shadow of the home of the President of the United States at Oyster Bay. The next day it is a judge in Paterson, N. J., slain by a bomb sent him by the Black Hand, while his son was all but killed. A Connecticut millionaire dies from anxiety brought on by the receipt of numerous Black Hand letters.

None seems to be safe. The society assails countrymen and outsiders alike. All who possess money form the grist that comes to the secret murder mill.

Work in the Dark.

Tony Sparbaro is a prosperous saloon-keeper at 183 Wells street. Mr. Sparbaro has saved a little money. He is called the "King of North Side Italians." A short time ago Mr. Sparbaro received a Black Hand letter demanding that he give up $2,000 cash to be deposited in a certain place under pain of death should he not do so. It was perhaps fortunate for Mr. Sparbaro that he was suffering from an attack of appendicitis at the time and was in a hospital. He did not "give up." He could not have paid threatening missive attention had he so desired.

Nicholas Bormeo is a hard-working Italian living at Gault Court and Oak street. He has saved a little money, and evidently some of his countrymen know it. A few weeks ago Mr. Bormeo was awakened at 3 o'clock in the morning by a knock at the door. Two men confronted him when he opened it. They handed him a letter. In it was a demand that he pay over $5,000 to a stranger whom he was to meet at Halstead and Division streets. The letter was written in Italian, and was signed, simply, "The Secret Five." He was warned not *to notify the police under penalty of vengeance. Mr. Bormeo said nothing to the police, but he decided not to be "bled."*

A few days later the men came again early in the morning and repeated their demand. Mr. Bormeo was given 24 hours to produce the money. This time Bormeo notified the police of the East Chicago avenue station. A watch was set for these blackmailers, but the latter were not to be caught. Several nights afterwards, as Bormeo was seating himself at supper, a shot was fired. A bullet broke the window glass and passed a few inches from Bormeo's head. There was the intent to kill him. Bad marksmanship was the only thing that saved Bormeo's life. He yet may be made the victim of Black Hand vengeance.

Slain While They Slept.

A crime difficult to surpass in fiendish cruelty and disregard of human life occurred near Chicago three years ago. It was laid at the door of the Black Hand. A "gang" of Italians were at work near Momence for the Illinois Central Railroad. They were engaged in construction work. Some fifteen or twenty of them occupied a portable shack near the railroad tracks. They were hard-working and saving men.

A peculiarity of the average Italian immigrant is that he trusts no one, and from an excess of caution sometimes overreaches himself. The Italian generally carries his savings with him in a belt around the waist. Three of the laborers had announced they would return to Italy after the next payday. The news was noised about. It was known that they had money. It was the cause of their undoing.

The Black Hands determined to reap where they had not sown. On the night after payday as these laborers lay upon the floor of the shack, the door was suddenly thrown open. Shotguns were discharged into the midst of the sleeping men. Four were killed outright. Some few escaped wounds to the outside. The murderers then went through the clothing of their victims, and after securing their savings set fire to the shack. The charred bodies of the Italians showed the deadly bullet wounds. The bodies had been "stripped clean" of all valuables. Six of the Italians were brought to the city and taken to the county hospital. Two of them died.

Case of Wholesale Murder.

Just a case of wholesale murder for a few dollars.

Again the police were at a standstill. Nothing in the way of solving the mystery was ever accomplished.

The terrible killing of Antonio Natalie horrified Chicago. Natalie lived at 193 Union street. He was of the usual hard-working type of Italian. He had accumulated a little money, at least that was his reputation. One day a barrel was found on the Prairie near Chicago and Western avenues. When the barrel was opened the mangled body of a man was disclosed. The head had been almost severed from the body and an attempt had been made to make identification impossible by marring the features. The body had first been placed inside a sack. The sack bore the mark of a Halstead Street merchant.

With this clue detectives Peters, Larson, Hamilton, and Kubisky of the West Chicago avenue station went to work. The merchant said he had given the sack to an Italian who lived in the vicinity.

Later Philipo Rine and Dominic Beamont were arrested, charged with the murder of Natalie. The latter had been killed for $300. Rine, when arrested, had the blood-soaked money on his person. These men were tried and sentenced to Joliet prison for life. That was one time when the police were successful in detecting the murderers.

Trunk mystery Is Solved.

This case was on a par with the famous Italian trunk mystery, which was solved by Lieut. Andrew Rohan, of the Central station. The attention of the police of Pittsburgh was called to a badly smelling trunk which no one called for at the railway station. The trunk was opened and found to contain the decomposing body of an Italian. It was learned that the trunk had been shipped from Chicago and in one way and another that the body was that of Filipo Carnso, who had lived in a house in Tilden avenue. Lieut. Rohan went to the house in the dead of night and arrested five Italians, who were locked up, charged with having killed Carnso. Three of the men were Ignazio Silvestri, Agostino Gelardi, and Giovanni Azari. Eventually these men confessed.

It seemed that Carnso had saved $500, and his countrymen determined to possess themselves of it. The men were in the habit of shaving one another. The plot prepared, when Carnso placed himself in the chair a rope with a running noose was deftly slipped around his neck, and with a man on either end, his life was strangled out of him. The body was then robbed and placed in a trunk purchased in a Madison Street store. Silvestri bought a ticket for Pittsburgh and the body was placed aboard a train in the trunk. Silvestri was afraid to call for the truck and went on to New York. Silvestri, Gelardi, and Azari were executed for the crime.

Dr. Nicholas Re, an Italian physician, owner of the drug store at 438 Dearborn street, had an experience with a Black Hand representative which Dr. Re persisted in regarding as amusing, but which to most persons would have seemed very serious. Here is Dr. Re's story:

I have an office in the rear of my store where I look after my patients," said Dr. Re, "One day I observed a pleasant looking young man who stood unostentatiously in the *corner of the waiting room. He waited until I got through with the patients, and then stepped into my private room, closing the door after him. I asked him what I could do for him, and you may imagine that I was a little surprised when the young fellow said in Italian:*

I do not come here for treatment, but I have come here to kill you.

Piece of Daring Blackmail.

It sort of took my breath away, but at the same time I cannot help laughing. 'Kill me?' I repeated. 'What do you want to kill me for?'

You must give me $500,' the young man said, and he then went on to say that if I did not give him $500 it would result seriously for me. I questioned him, and he told me that a good Italian friend of mine had offered $500 to kill me, but that if I would give him $500 he would spare my life. I asked him the name of the man, and he told me. I asked him if he had received the money, and he said no, that he was to receive it the next day. I told him that when he got the money to come and show it to me, and then I would talk business to him.

He went away and, of course, I got into communication immediately with the friend who was supposed to have hired the stranger to put me out of the way. The story proved to be false. But sure enough the next day the young fellow was on hand. I asked him if he had the money. He told me that he had not received it all, but that he had been paid $100 on account. I asked him to show me the $100. He brought forth a Confederate $100 bill. I laughed in his face and told him that the money was no account. He tried to argue with me. I laughed some more. He told me that I must not laugh; that it was very serious, and that I would surely die unless I gave him $500. I began to think by this time that there *might be something in it, and I put the fellow off, telling him to call the next day and I would have the money.*

I intended to hand him over to the police, but the man did not return. I did not see him again for a year, when I ran into him on the street. I had him arrested, but nothing came of the case, as a justice at the Harrison street police station thought that too long a time had elapsed to make a case against the man, and besides nothing serious had happened – just an effort to blackmail which was not successful.

Charles Bartholemie, 1228 Milwaukee avenue, however, did not play in such good luck. Bartholemie lost $7,328, supposedly through Black Hand agents. A man visited his store nightly for a month until he won the confidence of Bartholemie. A proposition was then made that the merchant take the alleged illegitimate daughter of an Italian nobleman and keep her until she was 18 years of age, for which he was to receive $3,000 when he accepted the charge and $10,000 at the end of the third year. In order to show good faith Bartholemie was to deposit $10,000 in the bank.

Bartholemie drew $7,328 that he had in a bank to deposit in another bank to make up the total. During the transfer he was accompanied by the agent, who suggested that they go to the Union restaurant and have lunch. At the restaurant the agent met a fellow countryman who was introduced to Bartholemie, and the three had lunch together. After the lunch the money was shown in a satchel. Suddenly the friend of the agent excused himself and almost immediately the agent also disappeared. Then Bartholemie looked in his satchel. He found nothing but paper.

The satchel had been switched – an old trick, but successful once more. The swindlers were never apprehended.

An Italian was found half dead on the West Side. He was shot four times and stabbed eight. A description of his assailants was furnished the police. The attention of officers of the Rawson street station was attracted to the peculiar walk of a woman who was crossing the North avenue bridge. She was arrested. Taken to the station as the proposed woman was found to be a man dressed in woman's clothes. The prisoner was taken to the hospital where the wounded Italian identified him as his assailant. After the Italians recovery he refused to prosecute. Later the man whom the police had arrested was found murdered in an Italian railway camp. Was it vengeance?

A Black Hand letter was received by Mettillio Pierone, a butcher, at 2228 North Halsted street the letter was an Italian attached were cabalistics in the form of a skull and cross bones, dagger, and cross.

We all of us thank you for the success that has happened, but for your security do that which we have written in the first and take good care of doing exact things and woe to you people if you do not deliver the said sum, more than the past $1,000 at the stated place. If you don't do this now within the term of a week, we will think of something else. If we will not succeed here in Chicago in the other parts even in hell. Even if you leave the city we will think to revenge ourselves with a severe vengeance and precaution.

THE MYSTERIOUS HAND

Secret Crimes in East.

The Black Hand crimes in the East have been numerous and terrible. The most prominent victim outside of Italian circles was David Wesson, the millionaire manufacturer of revolvers. A year ago he began to receive threatening letters from the Black Hand. At first he paid no attention to them. But one after another the small threats were literally carried out.

Mr. Wesson became worried, and anxiety soon developed into genuine terror. His death some months ago was laid at the door of the Black Hand. He left a fortune of $30,000,000.

Last January the Black Hand got to work in Oyster Bay, where President Roosevelt has his home. It was a crime of characteristic daring. After receiving no money in answer to their threats, the Black Hand agents dynamited the store of their victim, completely ruining it.

On February 8 last, Judge Robert Cortese, of Paterson, N. J., and his son Robert started to open a box sent by express to Mr. Cortese. It was sent him by the Black Hand, and after he had taken no notice of several threatening letters. Paterson criminals had feared him. The box was an infernal machine, which exploded, killing him and dangerously wounding his son. He left a widow and eight children.

The operations of the Black Hand extend to every part of the country. No one knows when he will receive one of their threatening letters, only to be followed by a terrible vengeance if heed is not paid.

Little doubt exists in the minds of the police that the Black Hand and other criminal associations are being recruited from members of such organizations in Italy. It is known that just at the present time the organization known as the Camorra is unusually active in Italy. Quite recently 500 Camorrist ringleaders were arrested in Naples as a result of the determined crusade undertaken by the government against those secret criminal societies. The Neapolitan prisons are reported full to overflowing, as many as twenty culprits being lodged in a single cell. On this account, and because the Camorrist were found to be holding committee meetings among themselves and regular communication with comrades outside by means of their own slang code, the authorities have now begun transferring them to different provincial houses of detention till the time of trial is fixed, which probably will not begin for another twelve months.

Despite elaborate precautions taken to effect his capture, Erricone, the notorious supreme chief of the Naples Camorra, has succeeded in reaching the United States, whence he dispatched a message to his pursuers, saying he had merely taken a sea voyage at his doctor's orders, and his absence from his post was only temporary. Erricone managed to board an emigrant liner in the disguise of a coal heaver, and cross the Atlantic as a stowaway.

The police feel that the presence of Erricone in this country creates a grave menace to the well-being of the community. No crime is too black, no exploit too dangerous for Erricone to undertake. He has never been known to work, and Americans and Italians will be compelled to furnish him with the means of subsistence. The Mafia or the Black Hand, it is feared, will become his nefarious agents in preying upon the public.

New York Tribune

Wednesday, December 28, 1910

BAD DAY FOR BLACK HAND

Maria Rappa And S. Pattenza Go to Prison for 25 Years.

DRAMATIC SCENE IN COURT

Judge Fawcett Deplores His Inability to Impose Death for Child Stealing.

Deploring his inability to impose the death penalty, Judge Fawcett, of the Kings County Court, yesterday morning sentenced Maria Rappa and Stanislao Pattenza to spend a term of not less than twenty-five years nor more than forty-nine years and ten months in prison for their part in the kidnapping of eight-year-old Giuseppe Longo. Less than three weeks ago the police had no proof of their connection with the disappearance of the boys. The rapid work of the authorities attracted as much attention as their success in securing the convictions. Half a dozen other members of the gang are at large, but the police know who they are, and expect to catch them in time.

The scene in court yesterday was unusually dramatic. The large room on the ground floor of the County Courthouse was jammed with humanity at 9:30 o'clock. There was a noticeable absence of Italians. Many of the spectators were said to be from Manhattan. Dozens of people who could not crowd into the room hung about the corridors and waited anxiously for the sentence. Interspersed throughout the crowd were many plainclothes men with their hands on their guns, ready for anything that might develop. It has been an open secret from the first that the authorities feared an attempt upon the judge or an effort to rescue the prisoners.

Judge Fawcett entered the courtroom at 11 o'clock. He was surrounded by court officers, and Chief Clerk Charles S. Devoy took his stand nearby. An intense hush fell over the crowd, when the order came: "Call Maria Rappa!"

Maria Rappa Enters.

Half walking, half carried by two stalwart court officers, the diminutive woman appeared at the door of the prisoner's pen. Her shawl was wrapped closely about her thin shoulders and her great black eyes, glaring with fear, turned excitedly from side to side. The fear of the crowd more than the fear of justice seemed to be upon her. She seemed to expect a bullet to come crashing out from among the crowd to her left. The officers hustled her quickly before the judge's bench.

"Maria Rappa," began the court, "have you anything to say why sentence should not be pronounced upon you?"

"What can I say!" she cried when the interpreter explained the question to her. "They wanted to convict me, and they did convict me. I know nothing about it."

"Maria Rappa," said the judge, "you stand convicted of the crime of kidnapping. You were a member of the Black Hand gang that kidnapped Giuseppe Longo and Michael Rizzo. It is almost unbelievable that you and your neighbor, Mrs. Castalla, could have held these two crying, brokenhearted children, knowing as you must have known, the terrible suffering of their distracted parents.

"You have given birth to children. Your own children lived with you in the very room where you kept Giuseppe Longo a prisoner. The part you have taken in this crime shows that you have not the spirit or instinct of a mother. The God-made mother love is better shown in beast and birds than in such as you. A good mother is the holiest thing alive, but you gave no evidence in any way of having any of the qualities of goodness. Mother is synonymous with love, but your heart never revealed any love to the little ill treated Giuseppe. The unnatural part you took in this crime stamps you as an undesirable member of society."

When the prisoner heard the period which she was condemned to spend at Auburn Prison she fell fainting into the arms of the officers, with a feeble scream in Italian of: "Oh, God!

Pattenza Swaggers In.

Hardly had she been removed when the same door opened to admit her fellow prisoner, Stanislao Pattenza. Showing his training in the Italian army, he swaggered in between the court officers, his face wearing the same smile of bravado with which he faced the jury that convicted him. He shook his head when asked if he had anything to say why should not be sentenced.

"Stanislao Pattenza, you are the chief of the Black Hand gang that kidnapped Giuseppe Longo and Michael Rizzo," declared the judge. "You threatened Francisco Longo, the father of Giuseppe, with death if you failed to get $15,000. Father and son had only two days longer to live, according to your letters, when the police rescued the boy and arrested you and Maria Rappa. The others in this conspiracy have made their escape, but they are known to the police and sooner or later will be apprehended. Your gang has now got to reckon with Deputy Police Commissioner Flynn, who *is as resourceful in detective skill as your vicious gang is in secret methods.*

"Maria Rappa would have made a confession in open court had not been that an emissary of your society called on her at the jail on the eve of her trial and informed her that if she revealed the secrets of the society she would be punished with the penalty of death. She knew how desperate your members were, and her tongue was still.

"You were the brains, the leader and acknowledged chief, the king of the Black Handers. You and the others live from the fruits of your dastardly crimes of kidnapping, bomb throwing and blackmail, your society during the last few years has caused a reign of terror among the good people of your race in this city. Criminals of your class should never have been admitted to the country. No worse men are allowed to live than Black Handers. Men of your habits should be punished as severely as those guilty of murder. I regret that the law does not provide the death penalty for such crimes."

As the court ordered the prisoner away to Sing Sing, a great sigh of relief and satisfaction went up from the crowd. The prisoner accepted the sentence without a word or a change of front. Intimations were given by the lawyers of the prisoner that they would try to secure writs of reasonable doubt and carry the case upon appeal.

The Courier Journal

Sunday, March 14, 1909

DIES A MARTYR.

Black Hand Detective Murdered in Italy.

LIEUTENANT PETROSINO, OF NEW YORK, ASSASSINATED.

SENT ABROAD TO FERRET OUT CRIMINMALS' HAUNTS.

DEATH WILL BE AVENGED

Palermo, Sicily, March 13.

Lieut. Joseph Petrosino, head of the Italian squad at the New York police headquarters, was shot to death at 9 o'clock last evening under the shadow of the trees of Marina Square, in this city. Whether he was lured there or not is unknown, but is believed that Petrosino, who, during his stay in Sicily, has been indefatigable in searching up the records of Sicilian criminals, had gone to the square in the hope of securing information which he considered of importance.

The identity of the assassins has not been disclosed, for they made their escape, after having made certain of the death of the detective. Not the slightest trace of them has yet been discovered, but undoubtedly they were men who had reason to dread Petrosino's presence in Italy, either because he was on their tracks, or on the tracks of fellow members of some of the secret organizations from America.

Petrosino had managed to collect while here much evidence of the criminality of the large number of Italians who have taken refuge in the United States, which would have given the American Government the power to deport them. In a number of cases Petrosino had traced murder to their hands. His work will be largely destroyed by his death, as he had not the time nor the opportunity to place much of his data on record.

Cold-blooded Murder.

His assassination was a most cold-blooded one. He was attacked in the darkness at the corner of the deserted square by two men, who fired three shots at him. Petrosino, though mortally wounded, clung desperately to life and showed at the very last moment extraordinary courage and coolness. Though the blood was streaming from him and he could feel that death was near, he clung with one hand to the grading of a nearby window. He managed to draw his revolver and fire one shot, then he fell to the ground. His bullet missed its mark, but the noise of the explosion attracted several passers.

The first of these was a sailor from the warship Calabria, who as he ran up saw the detective dragging himself to his feet and grasping the iron bar with nerveless hands, but as the sailor reached him, Petrosino fell again to the ground, covered with blood which was flowing from a desperate wound in the face. His eyes were still staring as, in a last effort to defend himself, he turned, revolver in hand to where his assailants had been. He was dead before the sailor and others who came to his assistance could raise his head.

Easily Identified.

A Magistrate, who was notified of the assassination, went immediately to the spot and ordered the body searched for identification. The identity of the murdered man was at once disclosed. From papers found on him it appears that he had been gathering evidence with reference to criminals in the United States.

There were also notes concerning the Palermo members of the Black Hand. Several postcards were found addressed to his wife, "Adelina Petrosino, 223 Lafayette Square, New York," and a metal badge, number 285. From other papers found on the body it appears that Petrosino had made a tour of Sicily and had given special attention to Trapani. The magistrate gave orders that the body be transported to Rotali Cemetery, where a post-mortem was held.

HAD BRILLIANT RECORD.

Petrosino a Terror To Italian Criminal Organizations.

New York, March 13.

No crime in years has so stirred the people generally and the police in particular as has the assassination of Lieut. Joseph Petrosino, of the New York police force, in Palermo, Sicily. By many, Petrosino is considered a martyr. He had received numerous threats that unless he ceased his efforts against the Black Hand, the Camorra, the Mafia, and other Italian conspirators and criminals, he would meet his end. Petrosino, however, was not deterred in the work he believed he was called on to do for civilization and humanity, though he prophesied to his friends the fate that befell him yesterday.

A relentless warfare has already commenced here and in many other American cities against the class of criminals who brought about Petrosino's death. Instead of stopping investigation and prosecution, as they had perhaps believed, the murder will cause only added activity on the part of the police all over the country, and it is hoped that it will result in closer co-operation between the Italian Government and our own in barring these criminals from the United States ports and in deporting many that are here now.

Splendid Record.

Petrosino was 48 years old and became a member of the Police Department in 1883. He was the "find" of Inspector Alexander Williams. Williams was attracted by the active and bright young Italian and conceived the idea of using him in the Italian colonies, where crime was frequent and hard to trace. From the first Petrosino was successful. His arrests have run into the thousands. While his convictions have been proportionately large. The Black Hand crimes had recently received much of his attention and his trip to Italy was in furtherance of his idea to establish secret bureaus there that would keep the police here informed when criminals emigrated to this country so they could be kept out.

He was also arranging whereby known Italian criminals now here could be deported, especially men or women who had sentences or charges hanging over their heads in Italy. In this work Petrosino had the hearty co-operation of the immigration authorities, of Police Commissioner Bingham and of many Italian businessmen. It was, in fact, the latter who furnished the funds for Petrosino's trip to Italy and the work he was doing. The Board of Alderman and the city officials having neglected to appropriate money for the purpose. Petrosino had been on his mission about two months and was about to return when he was assassinated.

Roosevelt Shocked.

Former President Roosevelt was one of those who knew Petrosino well and he was greatly shocked at the news.

"I can't say anything," he said, "except to express my deepest regret. Petrosino was a great man and a good man. I knew him for years and he did not know the name of fear. He was a man worth while. I regret most sincerely the death of such a man as Joe Petrosino."

Police Lieut. Antonio Vacheys, chief assistant of Petrosino's Italian criminal bureau of the metropolitan police, feels the death of his friend keenly and wants to avenge it.

"I feel certain," he said to-day, "that I can land the gang responsible for the death of Petrosino at Palermo. I know of nothing that would suit me better than to be sent over there with a squad of secret service men that is what must be done to avenge the death of our comrade, and I shall ask leave to go.

"Palermo is the worst hole in southern Italy for the Mafia. There are at least 100 criminals of the worst type who knew Petrosino, for many of them had been deported from the United States as a result of his detective work here."

Arranged In New York.

Men who know the methods of the Italian criminal organizations are certain that Petrosino's death was decreed in New York City and accomplished with military obedience by the Mafia, who are in league with the Italian criminals here. Inspector McCafferty, head of the New York detective bureau, besides sending telegrams broadcast to stir up activity against Italian criminals throughout the country, sent every available man he had to work in the Italian colonies in the city and its vicinity. He told the men of the death of their brother officer and said he expected from them speedy results.

Deputy Commissioner Wood late to-day sent the cablegram to the American Consul at Palermo requesting him to take charge of the body of the murdered detective until further arrangements are made for bringing it to this country.

THE ASSASSINATION OF JAMES GARFIELD

the 20th President of the United States

1881

AUTHOR'S COMMENTARY

There are very few crimes that reverberate worldwide more than the assassination of a President of the United States. Such a tragic and incomprehensible crime has a global impact.

There are thousands of historical newspaper accounts of the assassination of President Garfield. I have included a selection that I believe conveys the overall story. Note the time listed for the updates on the president's condition. Reporters were standing by at the White House, receiving briefings every few minutes. They, in turn, dispatched the information to their editors who quickly updated the newspaper. In today's media world, their rapid reporting was the equivalent of a twenty-four-hour cable network rushing to report every detail of a crime.

President Garfield served as a Major General for the Union forces during the Civil War. His Vice President and successor, Chester Arthur, served as a Union Brigadier General during the Civil War.

The Leavenworth Times

Sunday, July 3, 1881

HE STILL LIVES!

President Garfield Shot Twice

Yesterday in Washington

Chas. J. Guitteau Fires the Two Shots, Behind the President's Back.

The President at Once Receives Medical Attention and the Wounds Not Fatal.

He is Shortly Afterwards Removed to the Executive Mansion.

Sorry Reports of His Condition Until 9 O'clock Last Night.

He Then Rallies, and the Later Reports are More Favorable.

The Assassin Promptly Arrested and Conveyed to the Police Station.

He is a Disappointed Office-Seeker and the Probabilities are that He is Crazy.

He Also Attempts to Shoot Secretary of State Blaine, but Fails.

The Whole Country Ablaze With Excitement—Sorrow and Indignation Everywhere.

WASHINGTON, JULY 2

President Garfield was shot in the depo while waiting for the limited express on his way to Long Branch this morning.

9:30 A.M. – President Garfield was shot before leaving on the limited express this morning.

9:35 A.M – Col. Corbin has just passed in the president's carriage with the physician on the way to the Baltimore and Potomac depot.

NOT FATAL.

10: A.M. – Dr. Bliss says the president's wound is not a fatal one. President Garfield is now lying in a private room in the officers' quarters of the Baltimore and Potomac depo. Doctors Bliss, Surgeon General Barnes, Dr. Purvis, colored, are in attendance. The shooting was done by a slender man about five feet 7 inches in height. He refused to give his name, but it is said by persons who profess to know him that his name is "Dooty." The assassin was arrested immediately after the firing by the officers in the depo. He was first taken to police headquarters and subsequently removed to the district jail.

THE SHOOTING

occurred in the ladies' room of the depo immediately after the president had entered, walking arm-in-arm with Secretary Blaine, on their way to the limited express train, which was about ready to leave. Secretary Blaine, on hearing the pistol shots, two in number, rushed in the direction from which they came with the view of

ARRESTING THE WOULD-BE ASSASSIN.

Before reaching the man, however, the secretary returned to the president and found him prostrated. Both shots took effect, the first in the right arm and the second just above the right hip and near the kidney. The physicians have probed for the balls unsuccessfully.

The president is now being conveyed to the executive mansion, under a strong escort of Metropolitan police. Two companies of regulars from the Washington barracks have been ordered out to preserve quiet. Great excitement prevails, and the streets are thronged with anxious inquirers, eager to learn the condition of the president.

THE SHOOTING OCCURRED

in the presence of some fifty or sixty ladies. There is a rumor now that the shooting was done by ex-Consul to Marseilles,

Guiteau, who was removed from office. The pistol with which the firing was done is a California weapon, and extremely heavy caliber, better known as a "bull-dozer."

THE PRESIDENT COMFORTABLE.

The president has been made as comfortable as possible in his chamber at the White House, and all persons were excluded from the grounds in a summary manner. An immense crowd surrounds the grounds. The physicians attending the president are now holding a consultation. Various rumors are afloat; one is that the president is dangerously and another that he has been mortally wounded.

The president continues to improve.

ACCOUNT OF THE SHOOTING.

At half past 9 o'clock this morning when the president was at the Baltimore and Potomac depo with his party waiting to take the train he was shot twice by a man within 2 feet of him. The president's friends rushed to him as he fell, and Blaine called for Rockwell. Station agent Carney arrested the assassin, who said: "I did it; I am a stalwart, and Arthur is now president. Take a letter I have here to General Sherman, and he will tell you all about it."

The president's wounds are now said not to be mortal. There is great excitement.

WHERE HE WAS SHOT

The president was shot twice; one ball entered from the rear to one side and is believed to have passed through the kidneys. The doctors hold out some hope of possible recovery, but it is plain that they feel but little, if any, hope. One-shot went through the arm.

The president talked to a Western Associated Press reporter just now. He said he felt pretty strong, considering his wounds, but complained of a

TINGLING SENSATION

in his feet as annoying him more than anything else.

The man who shot him wrote his name on a card: "Charles Guitteau, attorney-at-law, of Chicago."

Washington is wild with excitement, and the whole populace is gathered about the Baltimore and Potomac depo. The man evidently had

DELIBERATELY PLANNED THE ASSASSINATION,

with the idea, so far as can now be ascertained, of making Arthur president.

The following official bulletin has just been issued:

EXECUTIVE MANSION, 12:36 P.M.

The reaction from the shock of the injury has been very gradual. He is suffering some pain, but it is thought best not to disturb him by making any exploration for the ball until after the consultation at 3 P.M.

(signed) D. W. Bliss, M. D.

President Garfield is conscious, and does not complain of great suffering. He has just dictated a telegram to his wife. It is impossible to say as yet what the result will be, but the surgeons are of the opinion that the wounds are not necessarily fatal.

TELEGRAM TO MRS. GARFIELD.

The following telegram has been sent Mrs. Garfield, at Long Branch; the president wishes me to say to you, for him, that he has been seriously hurt – how seriously he cannot yet say. He is himself, and hope you will come to him soon.

He sends his love to you.

(signed) A. F. Rockwell.

THE NEWS IN WASHINGTON

The news of the attempted assassination caused the most intense excitement in this city, and crowds surround the newspaper offices, all of which have issued extras. In the early part of the morning business was temporarily suspended on every hand. The latter favorable news that the president was not dead in a measure quieted matters.

THE DOCTOR'S OPINION.

Dr. Bliss, in attendance upon the president, says that the wounds are probably not mortal.

THE ASSASSIN.

The name of the assassin, as written by himself, is Charles Guitteau, and he says he is an attorney-at-law in Chicago.

The Star says, in an extra just issued, that when the assassin was arrested he said: 'I did it, and want to be arrested. I am a stalwart, and Arthur is president now. I have a letter that I want you to give to General Sherman. It will explain everything. Take me to the police station.'

HARD TO GET NEWS

It is utterly impossible to gain access to the white house, police and soldiers being all around it, and will not let anyone but cabinet officers in. There is communication by telephone, which is the only way to reach him.

The condition of the president is very much improved. Immediately after the shooting his pulse went down to fifty-three and his face, as he was removed to the white house, was of ashen hue. His pulse is now recovered to sixty-three, and the color is returning somewhat to his face. His

GENERAL SYSTEM,

moreover, denotes a very considerable improvement. It is not thought wise to make any further attempts at present to withdraw the bullets, and it is difficult to determine until a thorough examination is made how serious the internal injuries may be. Surface indications, however, give good grounds for hoping that the president will rally.

CHARLES GUITTEAU,

the would-be assassin, is a foreigner by birth. He has been a very persistent applicant for a consular position. He has haunted the executive mansion for several weeks, and his disappointment is not getting what he wanted led to temporary aberration of mind.

11:35. – President Garfield's strength is increasing every minute, and he is quite cheerful. The physicians announce that as soon as his pulse reaches seventy, another attempt will be made to probe for the bullet.

THE NEWS AT MEMPHIS.

MEMPHIS, JULY 2.

The news of the attempted assassination of President Garfield created great excitement in the city. Large crowds are now gathered on the streets and around the telegraph office, waiting for details of the crime. All classes are outspoken in condemnation of the dastardly act.

THE VICE-PRESIDENT.

NEW YORK, JULY 2.

Vice-President Arthur and Mr. Conkling arrived from Albany by boat this morning. The boat was late, not arriving until about 10 o'clock. As soon as she touched the wharf a telegram was handed Arthur. Upon reading it he dropped back in his chair, greatly shocked. It is presumed that the telegram announced the shooting of the president.

THE NEWS IN NEW YORK.

NEW YORK, JULY 2.

The news of the shooting of President Garfield reached the police headquarters simultaneously with the report that the president was dead. Amid the utmost excitement, the story fled from mouth to mouth, and was listened to at first with incredulity, but as a fresh confirmation of the rumor arrived indignation took its place. Mr. Nicholls, the only commissioner in the building, left hastily for downtown, in search of fuller information about the reported assassination. A total suspension of business in the department offices followed, the clerks and employees gathering in knots in the hall to discuss the situation, and to keep a lookout for fresh news. When, at length, a messenger came, announcing that President Garfield was not mortally wounded, a shout of "GOD BE THANKED!" went up from every side, and a sudden revulsion of feeling made more than one eye moist. The relief was so great as to produce a sudden disposition of unwonted hilarity; steady old clerks, who have gone at a tame gait for more than a generation, vaulted over desk and tables with the agility of boys and shook hands of joy. Business, politics, everything, were drowned in the common impulse of gratitude for the president's escape. Superintendent Walling struck his desk with his double fist a sounding blow, and shouted "Good!" in a voice that could be heard through the building. His venerable face fairly glowed with joy. From all sides was heard the one expression: "If President Garfield lives he will be the most popular president the country ever had." Along later, when the excitement had calmed down somewhat, came the particulars of the attempted assassination and of the murderer, that we received greedily. Business for the day was at end at the police headquarters.

ALARMING INDICATIONS.

EXECUTIVE MANSION, 12:30 P.M.

The president is somewhat restless, but is suffering less pain. Pulse, 112. Some nausea and vomiting has recently occurred. Considerable hemorrhage has taken place from the wound.

(signed) D.W. Bliss, M.D.

MRS. GARFIELD.

PHILADELPHIA, July 2.

The Pennsylvania railroad has ordered a locomotive and car at Jersey City to carry Mrs. Garfield to Washington. She had arranged to meet her husband at Jersey City today, and left Long Branch this forenoon on the Central road for Jersey City. The message informing her of the attempted assassination is awaiting her arrival at the latter place. There is much excitement here.

THE FEELING IN CINCINNATI.

CINCINNATI, O., July 2.

The feeling in Cincinnati is one of the mingled grief and rage in reference to the shooting of President Garfield. Cooler heads counsel moderation. Groups gather everywhere and make the awful event the only topic. The outcry against the leniency of communities towards crimes against persons as breeding the spirit of murder is everywhere emphatic and outspoken. The hope that the president will survive, coupled with the fear that he will not, adds suspense to the excitement and intensifies it.

INTERNAL HEMORRHAGE.

WASHINGTON, D.C., July 2.

2:20 P.M. the president's symptoms at this time are more unfavorable. It is thought that there is an internal hemorrhage.

THE CHANCES OF RECOVERY.

2:40 P.M. – Dr. Beckwith, an old physician of the president's, says that President Garfield has but few chances of recovery, that he may not live twelve hours. The general impression at the executive mansion is that the president is sinking.

DEATH VERY NEAR.

3 P.M. – Hon. Samuel Shellabarger, who has just left the bedside of the president, says that there seems to be absolutely no hope of rallying. His symptoms are growing more and more alarming and his death is thought to be very near.

THE NEWS IN ST. LOUIS.

ST. LOUIS, JULY 2.

The news of the assassination of President Garfield created intense excitement, and great indignation was expressed in every quarter and by all classes. Throngs of people gathered around the newspaper offices, where the bulletin was posted, and the extras, several of which were issued, were largely sought after.

THE NEWS ON WALL STREET.

NEW YORK, July 2.

The news down town was received with consternation, and caused much excitement on Wall street, Brokers and bankers almost forgot their business in their eagerness to get further particulars. They besieged Kernan's news agency, on Broad street, where dispatches from Washington were constantly arriving and being distributed. Groups were seen in the streets anxiously discussing the subject, and newsboys did a heavy business in extras. At the opening of the stock exchange the news depressed the market, but further dispatches announcing that the wounded president was in a fair way to recover, and was not as dangerously wounded as first reported, caused a reaction.

THE NEWS AT LONG BRANCH.

Long Branch, N. J., July 2.

So far the only particulars received of the shooting of the president is learned from the following dispatch:

EXECUTIVE MANSION, Washington, July 2.

Gen. Swain, Elbon, N. J.: We have the president safely and comfortably settled in his room at the executive mansion, and his pulse is strong and nearly normal. So far as I can determine from what the surgeons say, and from his general condition, I feel very hopeful. Come on as soon as you can; get a special. Advise me of the movements of your train and when you can be expected. As the president said on a similar occasion 16 years ago, "God reigns, and the government at Washington still lives."

(Signed) A. F. Rockwell.

THE NEWS CABLE TO ENGLAND.

WASHINGTON, D.C., July 2.

James Russell Lowell, Minister of London:

The President of the United States was shot this morning by an assassin named Charles Guitteau. The weapon used was a large-sized revolver. The president had just reached the Baltimore and Potomac station at about twenty minutes past 9, intending, with a portion of his cabinet, to leave on the limited express for New York. I rode in the carriage with him from the executive mansion, and was walking by his side when he was shot. The assassin was immediately arrested, and the president was conveyed to a private room in the station building, and surgical aid at once summoned. He is now, at twenty minutes past 10, been removed to the executive mansion.

The surgeons in consultation in regard to his wounds, pronounce them very serious, though not necessarily fatal. His vigorous health gives strong hopes of his recovery. He has not lost consciousness for a moment. Inform our ministers in Europe.

(Signed) JAMES G. BLAINE, Secretary of State

ABOUT GUITTEAU

WASHINGTON, D.C., July 2.

The librarian of the Navy Department has been before the attorney-general. He states that Guitteau was one of the supporters of those who made an effort to break the unit rule in the Chicago convention, and says that Guitteau was in the habit of calling at the librarian's room, telling how he had been treated by Secretary Blaine.

THE FOLLOWING PHYSICIANS

are in attendance at the executive mansion: Drs. Bliss, Ford, Huntington, Woodward, United States Army, Townsend, Norris, Purvis, Lincoln, Patterson, Surgeon-

General Barnes, and Surgeon-General Wales. A bulletin of the president's condition from the executive mansion will be telegraphed every half hour.

GENERAL GRANT—MRS. GARFIELD FRANTIC.

LONG BRANCH, July 2.

Gen. Grant has just arrived, and expressed deep regret at the attempted assassination of the president. Mrs. Garfield is almost frantic over the news. Her physicians allow her to see none of the dispatches, but dictate hopeful ones to her. A dispatch to Gen. Grant has relieved Mrs. Garfield's anxiety. It says that the president's wounds are not mortal. He is shot in the arm and hip.

GUITTEAU

CHICAGO, July 2.

Charles Guitteau, the man who attempted to assassinate the president, has been more or less known in Chicago for the past ten years. He was a disreputable lawyer, and has generally been considered half insane. He went to New York seven or eight years ago, and upon his return in 1876 professed to have been converted and delivered several lectures under the auspices of the Young Men's Christian Association. He next appeared at the head of a scheme to buy the Chicago Inter-Ocean, and run it on the plan of the New York Herald, but as he had neither capital nor backing the matter was soon dropped by him. He left for Washington several months ago.

A MORE DEFINITE ACCOUNT.

WASHINGTON, D.C., July 2.

The president had alighted from his carriage and was passing through the ladies' room to the cars. When about five feet inside of the room the assassin, who was within three feet of him, fired one shot. The president was dazed and made no attempt at self-protection. Blaine had turned toward a door as the assassin fired the second shot. In ten seconds the president fell, and Mrs. White, who attends the ladies waiting room, rushed to him and raised his head. Blaine also rushed to the assistance of the president.

The assassin passed out towards B street, but Captain Parke, ticket agent, jumped through the window and caught the assassin, who made no resistance. Officer Carney, depo policeman, rushed up and took hold of the assassin, and immediately afterward Officer Scott also took hold of him. Parke left the officers with him and turned his attention to the president. Help came in and the president was taken upstairs. He said not a word until he was laid down, when he asked that his shoes be taken off, saying that he felt pain in his feet. As soon as his shoes were removed he said to Secretary Windham: "Go right now and send a telegram to Mrs. Garfield, saying that I feel considerably better, and if she feels well enough tell her to come to Washington immediately." This dispatch was sent, and a special train was at once sent to Long Branch for Mrs. Garfield.

Secretary Blaine was not going with the party, but went down to bid the president goodbye. He said: "The president and I were walking arm-in-arm toward the train. I heard two shots, and saw a man run. I started after him, but seeing that he was grabbed just as he got out of the room I came to the president, and found him lying on the floor. The floor was

COVERED WITH THE PRESIDENT'S BLOOD.

A number of people who are around shortly afterwards have some of the blood on their persons. "I think I know the man; I think his name is Ditton." The assassin is about *five feet, seven inches in height, of strong though not stout build. The weapon he used was a revolver about seven inches long. It had an ivory handle; the calibr was very large. It is what is known as a California pistol. It made a very loud report. Parke says both shots were fired while the assassin was behind the president. When Officer Scott and Carney got hold of the assassin and were taking him to the police headquarters, he said voluntarily to them: "I did it, and I will go to jail for it; I am a stalwart, and Arthur will be president." He had a letter in his hand and wanted the officers to take it and send it to Gen. Sherman, saying it would be all right. The prisoner made no resistance, saying that he had contemplated the killing of the person, and it was for the good of the country.*

At 9 o'clock the assassin went to the hack-stand adjoining the depo, and engaged a hack from Barton, a colored hackman. He said he wanted to go to Glenwood Cemetery in short time, and wanted the hackman to drive very fast, when he should get into the hack. He agreed to pay two dollars for the hack, on condition that the hackman would drive fast. When stopped the assassin was going to the hack he had engaged, and he insisted that it was too important for him to go and deliver the message to Gen. Sherman. When the officer refused to let him go, he begged them to take the letter he had to Gen. Sherman. The following is a copy of the letter the assassin wanted delivered to Gen. Sherman:

July 2, 1881, – To the White House: – The president's tragic death was a sad necessity, but it will unite the Republican Party to save the republic. Life is a flimsy dream, and it matters little where one goes. A human life is of small value. During the war thousands of brave boys went down without a tear. I presume the president was a Christian and that he will be happier in Paradise than here. It will be no worse for Mrs. Garfield, dear soul, to part with her husband this way than by a natural death. He is liable to go at any time, anyway. I had no ill will toward the president. His death was a political necessity. I am a lawyer, a theologian, and a politician. I am a stalwart of the stalwarts. I was with Gen. Grant and the rest of our men in New York during the canvass. I have some papers for the press which I shall leave with Byron Anderson and his co-journalists, at 1420 New York avenue, where all reporters can see them. I am now going to the jail.

(Signed) CHARLES GUITTEAU

TELEGRAM TO ARTHUR.

WASHINTON, D. C., July 2.

Following telegram had just been sent from the executive mansion: Hon. Chester A. Arthur, Vice-President, New York City: At this hour–half past 3 – the symptoms of the president are not favorable. The anxiety deepens.

(Signed) JAMES G. BLAINE.

ANOTHER UNFAVORABLE BULLETIN.

EXECUTIVE MANSION, 4 P.M.

The following official bulletin has just been issued:

4 P.M. the president's condition is somewhat less favorable, the evidence of internal hemorrhage being distinctly recognized. Pulse, 130; temperature – 96. That is a little below the normal. He suffers rather more pain, but his mind is perfectly clear.

(Signed) D. W. Bliss, M. D.

PROBING THE WOUND.

Doctor Townsend, health officer, was the first to reach the president. The president was shot from the right as he entered the ladies' reception room of the depo with Secretary Blaine. The ball entered above the third rib, but whether it has taken its course towards the spine has not yet been ascertained. The wound was probed by Dr. Bliss, who reports that inserting the probe the ball did not extend toward the spine. Still it is not certain that it did not. It was the unanimous opinion of the physicians that the need for the present was not the probing of the wound, but rest. The extent of the danger of the wound is not yet known, and more can be told when the urine passes, if the kidneys are injured. The assassin is now in jail and many think he is crazy.

THE PRISONER.

WASHINGTON, D.C., July 2.

The district jail, in the eastern extremity of the city, was visited by an Associated Press reporter after 11 o'clock, for the purpose of obtaining an interview with Charles Guitteau, the would-be assassin of President Garfield. The officers refused admittance to the building, stating as a reason therefore that they are acting under instructions received from the attorney-general, the purport of which was that no one should be allowed to see the prisoner.

At first, indeed, the officers empathetically denied that the man had been conveyed to jail fearing it appears, that should the fact be known that he was there the building would be attacked by a mob. The information had reached them that such a movement was contemplated. A large guard, composed of the regulars from the barracks and Metropolitan police force, are momentarily expected to arrive at the jail, to be in readiness to repel any attack.

The statement that the assassin is Guitteau was verified by the officer in charge of the jail. The prisoner arrived and was placed in a cell about 10:30 o'clock, just one hour after the shooting occurred. He gave his name as Charles Guitteau, Chicago, Ill. In appearance he is a man about thirty years of age, and is supposed to be of French descent, his height is about five feet; five inches. He has a sandy complexion, and is slight, weighing no more than one hundred and twenty-five pounds. He wears a mustache and light chin-whiskers and his sunken cheeks and eyes far apart from each other give him a sullen, or, as the official described it, a "looney" appearance. The officer in question gave it as his opinion that Guitteau is a Chicago Communist, and he says it is a noticeable peculiarity of nearly all murderers, that their eyes are set far apart, and Guitteau, he said, was no exception to the rule. When the prisoner arrived at the jail he was attired in a suit of blue, and wore a drab hat, pulled down over his eyes, giving him the appearance of an ugly character. It may be

WORTHY OF NOTE

to state that some two or three weeks ago Guitteau went to the jail for the purpose of visiting it, but he was refused admittance on the ground that it was not visitors' day. He mentioned his name as Guitteau, said he came from Chicago.

When brought to the jail to-day he was admitted by the officer who had previously refused to allow him to enter, and a mutual recognition took place, Guitteau saying: "You are the man who would not let me through the jail some time ago." The only remark he made before being placed in the cell was that Gen. Sherman would arrive at the jail soon. The two jailers now guarding his cell, stated that they have seen him around the jail several times, recently, and he appeared to be under the influence of liquor. On one of his visits subsequent to the first one mentioned, these officers say that Guitteau succeeded in reaching the rotunda of the building where he was noticed examining the scaffold from which the Hirth murderers were hanged. Pursuant to his orders from the attorney-general, the officer in charge of the jail declined to give any further information, nor would he state in what cell the prisoner was confined. This officer was an attendant at the city jail at the time of the assassination of President Lincoln.

LATEST BULLETINS.

WASHINGTON, D. C., July 2, 5 P.M.

The president is a little easier and he suffers rather less pain just now. His mind continues unclouded, and he converses freely with those around him.

5:20 P.M. – Dr. Bliss says that the president is resting more comfortably, but his condition is very critical. Mrs. Garfield is expected to arrive about 5:45 P.M..

6 P.M. – The president has slept a few moments, but is manifestly weaker. Pulse, 140. He is mentally clear, conversing intelligently when permitted to do so.

(Signed) D. W. Bliss

BYRON ANDREWS' STORY.

WASHINGTON, D.C., July 2.

Byron Andrews, who is the Washington correspondent of The Chicago Inter Ocean, says that while it is true that a package of papers are in the hands of the police accompanied by a note addressed to himself (Andrews), he has no personal acquaintance with Guitteau and never heard of his existence until this morning. From what he has gathered from the police he believes that Guitteau is from Freeport, Illinois.

ANOTHER LETTER.

The following letter was found in the street shortly after Guitteau's arrest. The envelope was unsealed and addressed:

Please deliver at once to Gen. Sherman, or his first assistant, in charge of the war Department.

To Gen. Sherman: I have just shot the president. I shot him several times, as I wished him to go as easily as possible. His death was a political necessity. I am a lawyer, theologian and politician: I am a Stalwart of the Stalwarts. I was with Gen. Grant and the rest of our men in New York during the canvass. I am going to the jail. Please order out troops and take possession of the jail at once.

Very respectively, Chas. Guitteau

On receiving the above Gen. Sherman gave it the following endorsement:

HEADQUARTERS OF THE ARMY, WASHINGTON, July 2d, 1881, 11:25 A.M. – this letter was handed me this minute by Major Wm. J. Twining, U.S. Engineers, commissioner of the District of Columbia, and Major Wm. J. Beck, Chief of Police. I don't know the writer; never heard of or saw him to my knowledge, and herewith return it to the keeping of above–named parties, as testimony in the case.

(Signed) W. T. Sherman, General.

THE FEELINGS IN BALTIMORE.

BALTIMORE, O., July 2.

The most intense excitement prevailed throughout the city at the attempted assassination of the president. All business is suspended; the people are anxious and fearfully awaiting the results. Around the newspaper offices about Baltimore and South streets are blocked by crowds. The newspapers are issuing bulletins every half hour. There is a universal expression of indignation.

IN NEW YORK OFFICIAL CIRCLES.

New York, July 2.

At the sub-treasury and custom-house there was much excitement over the news, and great concern expressed for Gen. Garfield's recovery. Collector Merritt was found at the custom-house, surrounded by a number of gentlemen, and messengers were constantly arriving with the latest particulars. The collector was somewhat agitated, when asked for his opinion regarding the attempted assassination met the request with the question: "What's the latest?" When informed that the president would probably recover, he said he hoped so, and would not venture an opinion on the effect of the news, neither would he say whether he considered the attempt had any political significance, but merely remarked: "If the president dies, why, Gen. Arthur will be president." In the courthouse and other public offices the report created great excitement, and many speculations were indulged in as what would be the result of affairs throughout the country if Garfield should die and Arthur take the presidential chair.

GEN. ARTHUR AND SENATOR CONKLING.

Who arrived this forenoon from Albany, put up at the Fifth Avenue. The vice-president was found in the lobby of the hotel. He said he had not received any private dispatch in regard to the shooting and knew nothing more than was announced on the bulletins. If it were true, he said he felt exceedingly sorry for Mrs. Garfield, whose present state of health is precarious. Senator Conkling remained in his room and refused to be interviewed.

Edward E. Thorne, past grand master of Masons of the State of New York, was greatly depressed over the news. He expressed the deepest sympathy for the president's family, and thinks that even if the wound should not prove fatal, the shock to Mrs. Garfield in her present condition would be very injurious. He deplores the shooting as being one of the greatest evils that could happen to the country.

GUITTEAU A FRAUD.

ALBANY, July 2.

Thurlow Weed Barnes, of The Albany Evening Journal, says that Guitteau, the man who shot President Garfield called on him last October, and asked for chance to speak on the stump for the Republican national ticket. Guitteau said that he had been employed by the Republican state committee to do work at their rooms in New York, and that he was on his way there. Barnes questioned him closely at the time, and not liking his looks, told E. M. Johnson, secretary of the state committee, that he believed Guitteau to be a fraud.

Johnson made a memorandum and said that he would look into the case. Barnes was chairman of the county committee. Guitteau said he came from Chicago.

THE NEW YORK ASSEMBLY.

ALBANY July 2.

In the assembly after reading the journal, Murphy moves that house take a recess. He said that he made the motion in consequence of the terrible news received from Washington. He then referred to the progress of the victim from the towpath to the presidency, and that he said horror of the act just committed was too great for expression, too stupendous for adequate punishment. The majority of the house would mingle its feelings with the entire country.

DR. TOWNSEND'S STORY.

WASHINGTON, D.C., July 2.

Dr. Townsend, health officer of the district, in a conversation this afternoon, said: "I found the president when I arrived at the Baltimore and Ohio depo, about five minutes after the shooting occurred, in a vomiting and fainting condition. I had his head lowered, which had been elevated by the attendant, and administered aromatic spirits of ammonia and brandy to revive him. This had the desired effect, and the president, returning to consciousness, was asked where he felt the most pain? He replied in the right leg and foot. He then examined the wound, introducing his finger, which caused a slight hemorrhage. I undertook to have him moved upstairs from the crowd.

"After getting him there Dr. Smith and Purvis arrived, and upon consultation with them, it was decided to remove him to the white house. Dr. Smith and myself accompanied the president in the ambulance to the white house, where another examination was made and stimulant again administered. An ineffectual attempt was made to trace the course of the wound and at 12:20 the president suffering much pain. A hypdermic injection of morphine was administered."

Dr. Townsend left the president shortly afterward, somewhat revived. The doctor said at 2 o'clock this afternoon that he would not give an intelligent opinion as yet but pronounces the wound dangerous.

RINGING WORDS FROM GRANT.

LONG BRANCH, July 2.

Gen. Grant, in speaking about the attempted assassination, says: "If this is the outgrowth of Nihilism in our country I am in favor of crushing it out immediately by the prompt execution of the would-be assassin and his followers."

INTERVIEWING CONKLING AND ARTHUR.

NEW YORK, July 2.

A reporter called at the Fifth Avenue hotel this morning, about an hour after the receipt of the dispatch, and sent his card to the rooms of Vice-President Arthur and ex-Senator Conkling. Word was immediately returned that the subject of the president's assassination was too serious a subject to be talked of on a moment, and neither would be seen under any circumstances. The reporter saw Conkling in the hallway near his room a few minutes after, and when asked his opinion of the shooting he bade to be excused: "The news has found me so unprepared and overwhelmed with personal cares that it almost stunned me. May God grant that it may not be true. It is the most terrible incident in our history since the death of Lincoln. If it is true, then may heaven help our country." *Mr. Conkling turned away and went to his room.*

MURAT HALSTEAD,

is at present stopping at the Everett house, and this morning when the news was given him he was sorrow-stricken. He looked at the reporter for moment, and cried out that it could not be true. On receiving the assurance that the report had been substantiated by the official dispatches, Halstead turned pale and said, with tears in his eyes, that he must have time to think of it.

"My God! How can such a thing occur in a free country? We have no Nihilists here seeking to overthrow the government; we have had peace for many years, and are in the midst of it, and I cannot understand it. I can only pray heaven that it is not true." When Hallstead had finished he turned to a friend standing nearby, and walked away with him. His sorrow was extreme, for although his physique is magnificent he trembled violently and supported himself on the arm of his friend.

THE GLOOM IN WASHINGTON.

WASHINGTON, D.C., July 2.

Before the president was removed from the depo, this morning, no one was permitted to enter the building except those whose presence was absolutely required. By some unaccountable means the news was conveyed to the multitudes on the streets to the effect that although the president was not dead, he was mortally wounded. Then a gloom seemed to settle down on the city like a great pall, and the vast concourse of people waited patiently outside the depo for news from within. They reminded one strongly of the friends and relatives of a dying man, waiting in the ante-room to the chamber of death. The suspense was dreadful; businessmen and ladies, the faces pale with excitement and eyes bloodshot with straining, stared fixedly at the door of the depo and strove painfully to learn or divine something concerning the wounded man within.

At last the door was opened and some of the doctors came out. The throng pressed closely around them and begged for information. The medical man said: "He is not dead; he is not in any immediate danger, and in fact there are hopes of his recovery." The purport of these words were conveyed to all the people present and was transmitted from lip to lip.

THE CITY DREW A LONG BREATH,

and the excitement which had been at a white heat thus far, cooled off. Then there was a stir on the outer edge of the crowd, and the people were moved off right and left and every way. It was to make room for an ambulance, which had been summoned to transport the suffering president to the white house.

TENDERLY WAS HE BORNE

from the building to the vehicle, and quietly and gently was he laid on the mattress therein. Then the vehicle drove off slowly to the white house, followed at a respectful distance by the crowd. When he reached it he was borne inside, and was followed by the Surgeon General, Dr. Bliss, who had attended him from the visit, and other physicians. The friends of the wounded chief stood sorrowfully about him, and the doors were closed between him and thousands who stood in the highways and byways of the city awaiting tidings.

LATEST BULLETIN.

WASHINGTON, D.C., July 2, 7 P.M.

Secretary Blaine has just sent the following to Vice-President Arthur: "Mrs. Garfield has just arrived. The president was able to recognize and converse with her, but in the judgment of physicians he is rapidly sinking."

BUSINESS SUSPENDED AT THE DEPARTMENTS.

WASHINGTON, D.C., July 2.

At the departments business has been almost entirely suspended. All the cabinet officers have been during the entire day at the white-house, and also have many other officials. The sidewalks about the executive mansion are densely thronged with people, who anxiously await the bulletins which at frequent intervals are being posted at the gates.

MORE ABOUT GUITTEAU.

WASHINGTON, D.C., July 2.

Charles Guitteau, the assassin of the president, is a Canadian Frenchman by birth, and hails from Chicago. He came here in February, with recommendations from various parties in Illinois to secure the United States Consulship to Marseilles, France. He went in March to the well-known boarding house of Mrs. Lockwood, formally Mrs. Rines, 810 Twelfth street, and tried to secure board. Mrs. Lockwood did not like his appearance, and gave him an out-of-the-way room in hopes of getting rid of him. He pretended to know General Logan and others that boarded there. Mrs. Lockwood states that he acted strangely at times, and about the middle of the month, when she presented his bill, he could not pay it. He afterwards left the house, and Mrs. Lockwood received a note saying that he was expecting a $6000 position, and would soon pay the bill. Mrs. Lockwood showed the note to General Logan who said that the man was crazy.

Three weeks ago he met Mrs. Rickford, of Mrs. Lockwood's boarding house, on the street, and requested her not to say anything about the bill he owed, as it would hurt him in his efforts to secure his position. Mrs. Lockwood says that Guitteau was a great bother to Gen. Logan, so persistent was he in his efforts to secure that gentleman's efforts in his behalf. Since leaving Mrs. Lockwood's house he has been stopping at various places, but never at a great length of time, or the reason that he appeared to have no funds. He told one of the boarders at Mrs. Lockwood's that he expected to be appointed minister to France, but did not desire it to be known. Up to day before yesterday, when he registered at the Riggs house, Guitteau has been stopping for the last six weeks with no baggage but a paper box at 920 14th St.

MORE BULLETINS

WASHINGTON, D.C., July 2, 8 P.M.

The president is low and sinking. Pulse, 150, but conscious. The physicians say that he cannot live more than two hours.

8:30 P.M – The president is sleeping pleasantly, and is more comfortable. Pulse, 128, temperature, 98 – slightly above the normal; respiration, 23, and more regular.

D. W. Bliss, M.D.

9:20 P.M. – The president has rallied a little within the past three-quarters of an hour, and his symptoms are a little more favorable. He continues brave and cheerful. About the time he began to rally he said to Dr. Bliss: "Doctor, what are the indications?" Dr. Bliss replied: "There is a chance of recovery." "Well, then," said the president, cheerfully, "we will take that chance." The president is now sleeping.

A STARTLING THEORY.

WASHINGTON, D.C., July 2.

There is a theory which has many adherents that the attempted assassination was not the work of a lunatic, but the result of a plot much darker that has been suspected. It is cited in support of this theory that Guitteau arranged beforehand with a hackman to be in the readiness to drive him swiftly in the direction of Congressional cemetery, as he made his appearance on returning from the depo. In the meantime he placed a bundle of papers in the hands of a boy, with a view, it is maintained, to creating the belief in his insanity, in the event of his capture. Guitteau said, on his way to jail, that the president's assassination was premeditated, and he went to Long Branch for the purpose of shooting him there, and was deterred by the enfeebled and sad condition of Mrs. Garfield, which appealed so strongly to his sense of humanity that he came back without carrying out his intention. Those by whom Guitteau has been examined since the shooting say he shows no symptoms of insanity, and it is understood that the letter which has already been telegraphed addressed to "the white house" is the only document in the collection which supports the theory of insanity. It is reported that Guitteau had prompters whose description is in the hands of the police, and further developments are anxiously looked for.

RECOLLECTIONS OF GUITTEAU

CHICAGO, July 2.

There are many recollections of Charles J. Guitteau, which is his correct name, who lived here several years and acquired an unenviable reputation. He was at one time on the point of marriage with an estimable young lady on the South-side; but his character became known just in time to prevent such a calamity to the lady and her family.

Guitteau left town immediately after this for some months. A gentleman remarked: "I remember Charles Guitteau well. He was here two or three years ago, and seemed to have no visible means of support. He preached or lectured on religious and social subjects, upon which he was an enthusiast. He started in here as a lawyer, but failed, and then tried to lift himself into notoriety by lecturing on religion, one evening in each week. His card in the newspapers is produced to-day, and is a literary curiosity. He bored the newspapers by trying to get his manuscript printed. He failed also as a lecturer, and then began life as a tramp of the more respectable order. He was branded by the Hotel-keepers association as a dead-beat. In appearance he is an American of French extraction, thirty-

five to forty years old, of medium height, slender build, fair complexion, brown hair, French shaped mustache, and beard tinged with gray. His whole appearance was that of a dandified man of small mental calibre. He was unusually fond of notoriety, and would go almost any length to get his name in the papers. He was arrested here once for embezzlement. He got the idea in his head that he was fit for official position, and has been trying with all his power to get a consulate in Marseilles.

THE FEELINGS IN LOUISVILLE.

LOUISVILLE, Ky., July 2.

There is considerable excitement on the streets, and great anxiety to hear from Washington and New York. Impression is that the outlook for the country and for the South, especially, would be very much less bright with Arthur than with Garfield in the presidential chair; but there is no anticipation of any serious trouble in any event. Sympathy is expressed for Mr. Garfield and his family. Business is rather more quiet, but not to any extent disturbed.

THE NEWS IN PITTSBURG.

PITTSBURG, Pa., July 2.

The news of the attempted assassination of President Garfield has paralyzed business. Intense excitement prevails, and the streets are crowded with people anxiously waiting for the news.

THE ASSASSIN WAS FORMERLY OF MILWAUKEE.

MILWAUKEE, Wis., July 2.

The assassin of President Garfield was a former resident of the city, where he practiced law. His name, as inscribed on his old sign, is Charles J. Guitteau. He had an office at

395 Broadway, and claimed ten years' practice in New York and Chicago. Interviews with Judge Mallory and Harold Edmonds, Esq., both of whom knew Guitteau well, establish the fact that he was considered by the few who formed his acquaintance as either a very vicious person, or else one who is insane.

Mr. Harold Emmons a lawyer of the city, said in an interview: "I was quite well acquainted with Guitteau. His name is Charles Guitteau. During the winter of 1878 he had a desk in my office in the city, and attempted to practice law here. He had but little business, and seemed very poor. Though it was winter he went about with only a thin summer coat on. He was not a foreigner, as reported, but I think was of French descent. I used to regard him as a little insane. In that respect he had some theory in regard to the esoteric meaning of the Bible, and claimed that it was not generally understood aright. Sometimes he would set the whole day in the office and read the Bible. When I entered the office I saw him on his knees in prayer. He also published some pamphlets on religious subjects, which are kept for sale at the bookstores. He was a good deal at the rooms of the Young Men's Christian association, and took part in the weekly prayer meeting there. I regarded him as a harmless fellow, but very eccentric. He had some business after he left the city. Parties used to call for him occasionally in regard to matters they had entrusted to him."

Among those who know the gentleman is judge Mallory, and whose court he had practiced for some time. The judge stated that he was a tall, swarthy, ill-natured looking fellow. In the Municipal Court it was stated that he was known as the defender of vile women, and never was known to have a respectable client. He was in every sense of the word a pettifogger.

Another person who knew him well here was Adolph Aerdgren, a practicing attorney. He describes him as a dark swarthy looking individual, who is evidently troubled with hypochondria, and full of all manner of visions concerning every imaginable subject. While here he was busied a portion of the time writing a book on "Morals." His mind evidently went by contraries, for he was known throughout the city as a vicious, wild character. His place of business was, however, afterwards changed from Broadway to 117 Wisconsin St., where he remained several months. He finally left the city, having, it is understood, been debarred for practicing in the courts. The next place he struck was Chicago.

AUTHOR'S COMMENTARY

By the end of summer, Garfield was ravaged with high fevers, chills, and mental imbalance. His attending physicians employed their best medical knowledge, and by today's standards, their techniques would be considered torturous. They continued to probe his wound with various instruments and fingers increasing the size of the injury from three inches in length to a laceration which began at his ribs and extended to his groin. Medical records on his condition indicate the President was already suffering from an infection. With the massive new incision and continued probing, pus oozed from the wound, and gangrene took its toll. Soon he developed sepsis, which devastated his body and began shutting down his organs.

It was a miracle the President survived an agonizing eighty days after being shot. During his battle for life, he lost nearly eighty pounds and slipped in and out of consciousness and sanity. On September 6, the President was taken to a beach cottage at Long Branch, NJ, where he expired on September 19, 1881, Racked with excruciating pain which injections of morphine could not eliminate, the president painfully whispered his last words, "This pain, this pain," and slipped into death.

Dr. Bliss, the attending physician, pronounced him dead at roughly 10:35 PM, saying to Mrs. Garfield, "It is over." The cause of death was listed as heart failure, a ruptured splenic artery, and infection.

When the President died, Charles J. Guiteau was immediately charged with murder, and his trial began on November 17, 1881. His court-appointed attorney attempted to use temporary insanity as a defense, but Guiteau vehemently objected, claiming he was completely sane at the time of the shooting. He was convicted of murder and sentenced to death.

Weekly Public Ledger

Tuesday, July 4, 1882

GUITEAU HUNG.

THE MOST VILLAINOUS OF ASSASSINS GOES HENCE.

THE DROP SPRUNG AT 12:40 p.m.

Preparations for the Execution Well Carried Out.

End of the Darkest Chapter in American History.

The Proprieties of the Occasion Duly Observed.

His Last Prayer and Poem.

WASHINGTON, June 30, 9:45 a.m.

Guiteau was very restless during most of the latter part of the night, not sleeping more than thirty minutes at a time. Towards morning he fell into a sound sleep from sheer exhaustion. He rose a few minutes after five and breakfasted heartily at 6:30. When the cook took his breakfast into the cell, Guiteau told him to bring

HIS DINNER AT ELEVEN O'CLOCK

promptly. Dr. Hicks, who remained at the jail all night, was called into the prisoner's cell soon after he rose and held a conversation on religious subjects with him. At 8 o'clock Dr. Hicks saw the prisoner again, when he made a request to have a bath, and asked Hicks to go out and see the scaffold.

Guiteau desired to arrange with the warden to have the trap sprung as soon after 12 as possible. He also expressed considerable anxiety lest some accident should occur, and insisted that Hicks should see that

THE SCAFFOLD

and its appurtenances were all in proper condition. After Guiteau had disposed of these matters he read a poem composed by himself, which he calls "Simplicity, or Religious Baby Talk." After reading it alone he attempted to sing it, but broke down in the effort. Guiteau then talked for some time about his future. He remarked that his heart was tender. "I don't think," he said, "I can go through this ordeal without weeping; not because of any great weakness – for principal in me is strong – but because I am

NEARER THE OTHER WORLD.

I hold to the idea that God inspired me." Guiteau subsequently asked that in his books all complimentary remarks about President Arthur and his administration be eliminated. He then presented Mr. Hicks the books that have been companions of his lonely hours. He told Mr. Hicks that he wanted to offer the first prayer on the scaffold, saying that he (Guiteau) would then read his favorite scriptural passage, the tenth chapter of John, and then pray on his own account. Then he intended, he said, to read his poem, "Simplicity." He desired to have the execution so arranged that just as he uttered the last word the drop should be sprung.

John W. Guiteau arrived at the jail at 9 o'clock, and was followed in a few minutes by Warden Crocker. These two gentlemen, with Mr. Hicks, had a consultation as to the disposition of the body. At 9:15 the prisoner came out into the corridor and exercised for 15 minutes. He walked very briskly, making it very difficult for his guards to keep pace with him.

THE SCENE ABOUT THE JAIL

this morning is unique. The office of the jail has been given completely up to a large corps of newspaper reporters, and a squad of them are scribbling away on every table, windowsill and every projection that offers rest for the paper. Many newspaper reporters remained all night. The private office of the warden has been transferred temporarily to the telegraph office. At 9 o'clock there was a constant stream of persons pouring into the jail. The scene

OUTSIDE

was like that of some great gala occasion. Some enterprising colored men had erected booths from which they displayed lemonade, cakes and other refreshments to weary and thirsty people, who began before 9 o'clock to assemble in the road in front of the jail. Messengers speeding to and from the city and carriages bringing visitors to the jail kept a continual cloud of dust hovering over the roads that lie between the jail and the city.

At 10 o'clock Guiteau expressed a desire to take a bath, and a large tub was taken into his cell. At this hour no one but the deathwatch was with him. Guiteau nervously disrobed and bathed. It was quite apparent to the guard, who is closely watching his every movement, that his object in asking for a bath was simply to obtain some employment which might distract his thoughts from the dread contemplation of his approaching death. He evinced increased nervousness, and his uncertain movements, distract manner and marked tremor in his tone when he attempted to speak impressed the guard with the belief that he is rapidly weakening.

10:45 A.M. – The rotunda was thrown open at 10 o'clock, and the newspapermen at once flocked in, there being but few others there, except the jail guards and a squad of artillerymen, who looked down upon the scene from the high steps leading to the scaffold.

Early this morning the prisoners in the part of the jail overlooking the court where the gallows stands were removed to another quarter and locked in cells. At 9 o'clock this morning the jail officers had a sort of rehearsal of the parts they are to play in the execution, chiefly for the purpose of testing the appliances of the gallows.

TESTING THE ROPE.

A bag of sand weighing 160 pounds was attached to the noose, the trap was sprung by means of the trigger rope, which was passed into one of the cells of the north wing, and the rope on the scaffold stood the test well.

At 10 o'clock Dr. Hicks and John W. Guiteau went with Gen. Crocker to the scaffold with a number of guards, and John W. Guiteau ascended the steps and carefully examined the structure, handling the rope and carefully inspecting all the fixtures, both above and below the platform.

A telegram from New York, signed J. D. Bunnell, was received about 10 o'clock this morning by Dr. Hicks, in which it is asked if the sender could obtain possession of Guiteau's body to be exhibited for the benefit of the Young Men's Christian Association. Dr. Hicks paid no attention to the message.

The order of procession to the scaffold, as agreed upon this morning, is as follows: Warden Crocker and one of his officers will appear first, followed by Dr. Hicks; then will come the prisoner, in charge of two guards, Coleman and Woodward. Behind them will walk, two by two, Jones and Hudson, and Johnson and Crocker for jail officers, the latter a brother of the warden.

PRECAUTIONS.

At 10 o'clock seventy policemen arrived at the jail, and were posted along the roadway outside the building. In addition to the regular jail guard all the available men of Battery C Second United States Artillery, are now on duty inside the jail.

Shortly before 11 o'clock Guiteau called for paper, and for twenty minutes busied himself in making a copy of what he terms is prayer on the scaffold. As his hands will be pinioned, Dr. Hicks will hold the manuscript while Guiteau reads. Now that he is employed, he appears

MUCH CALMER,

and is rapidly completing his work, writing in a large, round and legible hand.

At 11 o'clock, contrary to general expectations and her purpose as announced yesterday, Mrs. Scoville arrived at the jail and sought admission. She appeared to be laboring under great excitement. General Crocker declined to admit her unless the prisoner specifically requested it. John W. Guiteau, who was setting in the rotunda at the time, was informed that his sister was on the outside, and at first started to go to her, but after a few moments hesitation decided not to interfere, saying, "I will leave the whole matter with General Crocker." Guiteau has not been informed of

MRS. SCOVILLE'S PRESENCE,

and even if he was aware that she is here, it is believed he would not desire to have her present. His great desire now seems to be that there shall be no scene, and his programme *shall be carried out without any interruption or incident to detract from the heroic picture which he believes he is about to present.*

At 10 o'clock there was a large crowd of newspaper correspondents crowding about the gate leading into Guiteau's corridor, but they could see nothing except the wooden door which screens Guiteau's cell from view. Now and then a guard appeared at the door and sent some message to the warden. As such times those at the gate got a view of the table, corridor and chair on which the deathwatch sat.

After Guiteau had finished copying his prayer upon "The Scaffold," he began to arrange his dress, putting on a pair of navy blue trousers. At 10:30 the guard came out of the door and said: "He is ready for Dr. Hicks now and wants flowers to come." Another guard who took the message hurried off and soon returned with Dr. Hicks, who went into the cell. Guiteau was then reported by his guard to be apparently very composed. Guiteau's

MESSAGE ABOUT FLOWERS

referred to his expectations that Mrs. Scoville would send some flowers to him, but none had arrived at the jail at the time he asked for them.

After a short conference with Warden Crocker, John W. Guiteau went outside the jail to see his sister. He found her in great excitement, bordering on hysterics, but after a short time he succeeded in calming her, and dissuading her from any further attempt to gain admission. She acknowledged the propriety of such a course, but said she could not possibly remain in the city during all the wretched hours of the morning. She brought with her some flowers, which Guiteau had asked her for, and they were taken to the prisoner. Mrs. Scoville also brought two handsome flower pieces, a cross and an anchor which she will place on her brother's coffin with her own hands.

11:33 A.M.

While Dr. Hicks was in the prisoner's cell, at 11 o'clock, Guiteau made some request as to the execution, and having made copies of his "Last Prayer," poem, and other writings, tore up the originals. He then sent for the jail bootblack and gave him his shoes to be shined. His dinner was brought as the doctor was leaving, and he ate with much relish. His dinner consisted of a pound of broiled steak, a dish of fried potatoes, four slices of toast and a quart of coffee. Dr. Hicks, when he came out of the cell, said: "The prisoner has not the slightest fear. We have had a pleasant religious talk. He feels now that he is prepared, and is ready for the last formality. He commits himself to his God with the utmost confidence. I think he will show some emotion, because the nervous strain is so great."

Nobody but Dr. Hicks had seen the prisoner at this time, except the jail officers. At 11 o'clock Dr. A. E. McDonald, of New York, and Dr. Francis Lemay, his city expert witness at the trial of Guiteau, arrived at the jail. Dr. McDonald said that as he understood it, an autopsy would be performed by the three physicians agreed on by the friends of the condemned man; afterwards, the brain would be removed for further examination. The three physicians selected to perform the autopsy are: Dr. Lamb, who made the autopsy of the president, Dr. Sauers and Dr. Hartigan, Deputy Coroner of this city. Dr. Loring expects to make a thorough examination of the prisoner's eyes.

THE PRAYER.

The following is a full text of Guiteau's prayer as he has prepared to read it: "Father, now that I go to thee. Savior, I have finished the work Thou gavest me to do, and I am only too happy to go to Thee. The world does not yet appreciate my mission, but Thou knowest. Thou knowest Thou didst inspire Garfield's removal, and only good has come from it. This is the best evidence that inspiration came from Thee, and I have set it forth in my book that the President is a coward and an ingrate. His ingratitude to the man that made him and saved his party and land from overthrow has no parallel in history, but thou Righteous Father, will judge him. Father, Thou knowest me, but the world hath not known me, and now I go to Thee and the Savior without the slightest ill will toward a human body. Farewell, ye men of earth!"

Shortly before 12 o'clock Guiteau seemed to break down completely, and burst into tears and sobbed hysterically. Dr. Hicks sat by his side, fanning him and vainly trying to calm him.

About 11:30 preparations began to be made for the execution. At 11:50 a detachment of artillery was formed on the east side of the rotunda and brought their muskets to a parade rest. At that time about 250 people were in the rotunda. Dr. Hicks was with the prisoner engaged in prayer.

The crowd outside the jail have got word that Guiteau has been hanged, and they are rending the air with shouts, so that it is impossible to hear a voice inside the jail office.

Guiteau's neck was broken by the fall, and not a movement of the limbs or body was detected. Death ensued instantly.

SHORT CRIME STORIES

Crooks, Cons, Highwaymen, Desperados, and Editorials

AUTHOR'S COMMENTARY

A staple of newspaper reporting has been the short "filler" story. These "fillers" needed to meet a few standards while unintentionally providing us a glimpse into societal norms of the time. The editor considered these questions: Why is this story worthy of inclusion? Would it interest our readers? And most importantly, will the "filler" help sell newspapers? Printed media still employs the identical standard for selecting stories—large or small. Will the story sell newspapers?

In the simplest of terms, short stories provided filler material for leftover space on each page. And if it grabbed the attention of the reader, it served its purpose.

Today, considering the speed of digital media, many of these short stories would generate national or even international attention within hours, if not minutes, and continue for days. Consider the following headlines: Two Girls and a Man Hanged, Father and Daughter Murdered and Cremated, Two Students Shot, 34 Chinese Murdered, Girl Passes Death Sentence on Rapist, Murder Victim Chopped to Pieces, and A Girl's Lie Causes a Boy's Murder.

In today's world, these headlines would still be considered shocking. These short stories also illustrate an interesting sampling of crimes from the period. In many instances, identical crimes are perpetrated today. Others have given way to the ever-expanding new crime types of today which can be perpetrated digitally and via the Internet.

Unfortunately, as "fillers," it is rare to locate a follow-up story, which makes it very difficult to know if justice was eventually served.

It must be noted that the publisher and author do not endorse the language used to reference African Americans and other races in a derogatory manner. The articles were not included for their salacious language. They were included to demonstrate how African American people were viewed at the time by the public and media. It is clear members of the media freely included their racist views in the articles they wrote. It is hoped these articles serve as a teaching tool to all and clearly demonstrate the suffering and hardships free slaves and other African Americans were forced to endure for generations. Americans of all races must learn from history and work to erase racism from our country. It will not be easy, but we can do it.

St. Joseph Gazette Herald

Saturday, January 4, 1902

DENTIST DECLINES TO PERMIT WOMAN TO HORSEWHIP HIM

PAOLI, Ind., Jan. 3.

Paoli has been the scene of intense excitement today. It was announced that Dr. C.D. Driscoll, a dentist, would be publicly horsewhipped by Miss Eva Miller, a young woman who formerly resided here, but who at present is a clerk at Saltillo, a small town northeast of this city. She charged that the dentist wrote her an insulting letter.

Driscoll was arrested on a charge of alleged ill-treatment of his family. He was taken to his office. Then the fire alarm was sounded and the larger part of the townspeople gathered to see the whipping.

As they attempted to enter Driscoll's office the young woman and the officers with her were confronted with two revolvers which Driscoll flourished.

He said he would not be taken alive, and until late this evening he remained behind barricaded doors.

Finally, however, Driscoll was persuaded to come out on the street, after being assured that Miss Miller would be satisfied with a public apology and surrounded by an angry mob of incensed citizens, he apologized to the young lady for writing the letter.

The object of the mob's decision was then given twenty days in which to close up his business and leave the community.

AUTHOR'S COMMENTARY

This is perhaps the most insane editorial I located during my research. At first, I thought it must have been a form of cruel and sarcastic satire. However, after reading additional editorials from The Abbeville Press and Banner, and other publications, it became clear this editorial was not in jest. Although stated differently in other publications, the heart of other editorials was the same—pure hatred of African Americans and reinforcing the belief they were subhumans not worthy of justice.

From conducting years of research into the late 1880s, I thought I understood the depth of racism within the country; yet this editorial shocked me. It provided direct evidence of the unimaginable racism embraced by the news media of the time.

The Abbeville Press and Banner

Editorial

Wednesday, July 29, 1885

A Needed Law.

Some time ago we suggested that we have "a close season," say from the first of March to the first of October, during which time it should be unlawful to kill negroes. It really seems that the negroes are entitled to as much protection as is accorded to the different kinds of wild game. This protection is needed not so much on account of the negro himself, as on account of the evil effects resulting in the reduction of the crop products.

The killing of negroes between the first of March and the first of October to any great extent, is, in our opinion, highly reprehensible, and will interfere with the making of all kinds of crops, and hence seriously retard the material development of the country. In our humble judgment a penalty should be affixed for the crime of killing a negro, just as there is for killing a deer, or a wild turkey. If such a law existed and was enforced we think this sudden murderous outbreak in the killing of negroes in July, before the crops are gathered, might be averted.

Another matter, which we think deserves attention, is the fixing of bail by our Supreme and Circuit Judges. The idea of a Supreme Judge fixing the bond of the slayer of a negro in July, and in the midst of the crops, at twenty-five hundred dollars is opposed to the public policy of the country. In fact, it seems to us that it would be more in accord with the dignity of the office of a Supreme Judge if that officer should refuse, until the crops were gathered, to admit to his presence any man who had yet the smell of negro blood on his hands. There seems to be no earthly use in killing a negro in July. Those persons who may be interested in the distribution of the crops usually have some pretext for killing in the fall the negro who made his crops. The negro, as a rule, wants some portion of the crop which he has made and when he insists on any part of it, then it is perfectly right, and the white man is perfectly justifiable in killing him. He may feel entirely safe from punishment by law, if he secures the services of his "peers" at the trial, and the history of the past tarnishes an evidence of the promptness with which a jury of his "peers" will exonerate him from all blame in killing an impudent negro for claiming part of the crop had been made by his own labor.

If our Supreme and Circuit Judges would refuse bail to men who kill negroes during the crop time, they would certainly do much to postpone their killing until the "open season." As we believe nine out of ten killings of negroes is deliberate, willful, and malicious murder, these people could very well afford to put off the killing until after the crops are gathered.

As a rule gentlemen seldom find any inclination or necessity for the killing of a neighbor, and when a man kills another, it may be safely set down, that he belongs to a class of citizens to whom neither the Supreme Court, not the Circuit Judges, nor the peace-loving citizens of a community are under any special obligation. As these people voluntarily kill their neighbor, they should at least be compelled to lie in the jail until Court, or else wait unit the sitting of the Court, to do their killing, so that they may have an immediate trial.

We see it stated that some hanging is needed in our neighboring county of Laurens. We fully believe that there is absolutely no protection to life in that county, and if the law is never to be enforced, we should have good reason to fear the same condition of affairs in this county. Abbeville county needs some wholesome enforcement of the law, if any country on the face of the earth ever needed it. And it remains to be seen whether our jurors will perjure themselves and turn this country, soul and body, over to the rule of desperadoes and pistol-carrying gentry, who do continually set the law and decency and order at defiance.

If our memory serves us correctly no man has ever suffered for killing of any negro in this county or in this Judicial District, and we presume scores of negroes and white men too, now sleep in their bloody graves because our jurors disregard the peace and good order of society and wash the gore from red-handed murderers—sending them free to hunt another victim, and to further insult the respectability of our people, and with more deliberation, and, if possible, with more devilish atrocity, set aside the laws of the land, and trample under foot the shield which the law in its cowardice, and in its shame refused to extend to the humblest of its citizens.

The following four stories are from The Lindsborg News Record.

Friday, October 14, 1892

Murder and Arson

FATHER AND DAUGHTER MURDERED AND CREMATED

A HORRIBLE CRIME LAID AT THE DOOR OF A GANG OF

ALABAMA NEGRO DESPERADOES

MOBILE, Ala., Oct. 11.

Hacked to pieces with an axe and then cremated was the awful fate of Richard L. Johnson and his charming daughter.

A gang of desperate negroes is supposed to have committed the horrible crime. The tragedy occurred at Johnson's plantation, near Davis Ferry, Monte county, Friday night. There are no telegraph lines near the place and the news of the awful butchery, did not reach here until yesterday.

That there was a terrible struggle in front of the house there can be but little doubt. The sod is torn up and bloodstains cover the grass for several rods from the front entrance to the house. Just how it occurred, unless some of the ferocious blacks confess, cannot be told.

It was about midnight Friday night when the neighbors were attracted to Johnson's house by fire, which was coming out of the roof. The house was burned to the ground in the morning the charred bodies of Johnson and his daughter were found.

TWO STUDENTS SHOT.

Kansas University Men Killed with Shot for

Alleged Trespassing.

LAWRENCE, Kan., Oct. 11.

Late last evening Fred Bassett shot and dangerously wounded W.E. Higgins and Jack Cracroft. The shooting was done because the young men had crossed a tract of land Bassett had ordered them to keep off. Both were members of the Kansas university foot ball team and were on their way home from a practice game. The shooting was done with a repeating shotgun, and Higgins' wounds are very serious, his left hand and arm being torn to pieces, and a number of shot lodged in his body. Cracroft will recover all right, his most serious wounds being in the right knee and leg.

Young Bassett is a son of Judge O. A. Bassett, who made his headquarters at Salina for several years. He is about 18 years old. He was at once arrested and taken to jail. He acknowledges the deed but gives no cause for it but that the men shot were trespassing.

Double Murder and Arson.

DO, O., Oct 11.

On Saturday the house of Mr. and Mrs. Lucky in Kitley township was destroyed by fire and their bodies and that of their daughter were found in the ruins. It is now ascertained that they were murdered and the house burned to hide the crime. A son of the dead man who had been absent some years and had only recently been released from prison, where he served a term for burglary, has been arrested at Smiths Falls charged with the murder.

Two Girls and a Man Hanged

SPARTANBURGH, S. C., Oct. 8.

John Williams, colored, who killed J. A. Henneman, mayor of this city, September 27, 1891, and Millie Brown, a 15 year-old colored girl who killed the 1-year-old infant of W. C. Carpenter of Gaffney City, this county, in June last, were hanged on the same scaffold here to-day at 11 o'clock.

NEWBERRY, S.C., Oct. 8.

Anna Trimble, an unmarried colored woman, was hanged here to-day for the murder of her infant February 23.

East Oregonian

Thursday, February 15, 1912

GIRL PASSES DEATH SENTENCE ON RAPIST.

Memphis, Tenn. Feb. 15.

Identifying an unknown negro as her assailant, 15-year-old Kate Hodges was given the privilege to fix the fate of the fiend, by the mob that caught the black near Raleigh, Tennessee, where the assault occurred.

The girl decided that the negro should be hanged, and the mob carried out her wish, adding several hundred revolver shots, with which the rapist body was riddled as it dangled from a bridge.

Lloyd's Weekly Newspaper

Sunday, May 3, 1896

HORRIBLE OUTRAGE IN SPITALFIELDS

Spitalfields was yesterday morning the scene of one of the most atrocious and barbarous outrages that have ever disgraced that quarter of the Metropolis. About 8 o'clock Mr. Isaac Bryan, a greengrocer, of 110, Hansberry street, went to a stable as usual to attend to his horses. On opening the door he was startled to see a great quantity of blood about, and looking for the cause he discovered that a valuable animal was laying on its side with its head in a great pool of blood. He had once sent for the police and a veterinarian surgeon, who on arrival found that the poor creature had been horribly treated, its tongue being cut out close to the roots. No sign of the removed tongue was to be found, and it is concluded that the miscreant or miscreants concerned in the outrage carried it away. In the next stall another valuable horse was discovered evidently in great pain, and a little further on in the stall attended by Mr. Hard, of 4, David's -Terrace, Hunt St., lay a fine animal, the property of the latter gentleman dead.

In the last two cases the veterinary surgeon found that a corrosive poison had been forcibly administered, and the agony of the animals must have been very great. No reason can be assigned for these cruel deeds, and whoever performed them forced their way into the stable through a loose grading.

The mysterious part of the business is that the tongue cut from the first horse cannot be found, and it is stated in the neighborhood that this is the fourth outrage of the kind that has taken place, and each of the others horses tongues being cut out and carried off.

The case is in the hands of inspector Payne, of Commercial-street police station, and with his colleagues he is using every effort to discover the author or authors of this mysterious and brutal crime.

Buffalo Evening News

Saturday, September 10, 1881

A Girl's Lie Causes a Boy's Murder.

A Tombstone dispatch says: – In Ramsay's Canyon in this city a 13-year-old girl informed her father that in passing a Mexican woodcutting camp she had been insulted by a Mexican boy. A mob went to the camp and compelled the Mexicans, nine in number, to whip the boy with knotted rawhide thongs, resulting in his death a few hours later.

The girl subsequently said her story was not true but told for fun. Retaliation is feared from the Mexican side.

Daily Concord Standard

Tuesday, January 3, 1899

More Than "Jack the Ripper."

Joseph Vacher was beheaded in France on Saturday, the 31st. He was more than White Chapels "Jack the Ripper." In America he would probably have been pronounced insane, which he feigned after he was caught and confined. He had a kind of shrewdness in escaping detection and must have suffered a kind of mania for killing and carving up people. He was but 29 years old but has scored at least 22 homicides besides once shooting himself. Most of these crimes would never have been discovered but for a vein of pride that led him to tell of them himself when his story was always corroborated.

Laredo Weekly Times

Sunday, January 1, 1911

NEGRO RAPIST HID IN FIREPROOF SAFE

By United Press.

Wheeling, W. Va., December 22.

William Furby alleged to have made a criminal assault on Miss Angalin, near Weston, would have been lynched by a mob clamoring for his death had not officers secreted the prisoner in a fire and burglar-proof safe belonging to an insurance company, loading it on a train, as if it was in the ordinary course of insurance business, and shipping to this city, where he was placed in the penitentiary for safekeeping until the time of his trial.

Arizona Republic

Wednesday, December 16, 1903

TAKING OF A MURDERER

He Was Dead When They Got Close

Enough to Touch Him.

Spokane, Wash., Dec. 15.

With a posse hot upon his trail, Joe Dilio, the fugitive Italian murderer, left the road this morning and took refuge in the brush near Valley, Washington. Here he was discovered shortly after daylight. As the posse advanced through the brush, Dilio, who was lying behind a log, raised his head and pointed a revolver at his pursuers. The posse waited for no further warning, but opened fire riddling him with rifle bullets. Death was instantaneous.

Dilio and Antonio Del Vecchio were partners in a grocery store and saloon in Spokane. On Saturday they quarreled and Dilio shot Del Vecchio fatally wounding him. Dilio then fled.

Los Angeles Herald

Wednesday, September 30, 1891

WHOLESALE SLAUGHTER

THIRTY-FOUR CHINESE MINERS

MURDERED FOR GOLD.

Their Bodies Thrown Into Snake River.

A Band of Cowboys the Perpetrators

Of the Crime—The Identity of

the Murderers Just Disclosed.

SAN FRANCISCO, Sept. 29.

The mystery surrounding the finding of the bodies of twenty Chinese in the Snake River, Idaho, in 1889, has been solved. The bodies all bore gunshot wounds, showing that they had been murdered. The Chinese consul instituted an investigation, but was then unable to find who committed the crime. Consul Bee now makes public the following statement:

> I, Hugh McMillan, now of Walla Walla, Washington, but formally of Ininaha, Wallowa county, Oregon, make the following statement to the end that justice may be done to interested parties: I make the statement from a statement made to me by my son Robert, aged 16 years, just prior to his death, and by me then reduced to writing.
>
> In the latter part of April, 1887, my son and Bruce Evans, J. T. Canfield, May Larue, Frank Vaughn, Hiram Maynard and Carl Hughes were stopping in a cattle camp four miles from the Snake River. My son and Evans, Canfield, Larue and Vaughn went to a Chinese camp on the Snake river. Canfield and Larue went above the camp, and Evans and Vaughn remained below. The whole party was armed with repeating rifles and revolvers. There were thirteen Chinese in the camp, and they were fired on by the party above the camp. The unarmed Chinese retreated when they were fired upon by those below the camp. Twelve Chinese were instantly killed, and one other caught afterwards and his brains beaten out. The party got that evening $5500 in gold dust.

'Next day eight more Chinese came to the camp in a boat. They were fired on and all killed and their bodies, with the others, thrown into the river. The party then took the boat and went to another Chinese camp four miles distant, where thirteen Chinese were working on the river bar. They were all shot and killed and their bodies thrown into the river. The camp was robbed and $50,000 in gold secured. My son was present only the first day, but knew the facts, as they were talked over by the parties in his presence. Circumstances detailed occurred on the Oregon side of the Snake river, in Wallowa county, near the northeast corner of the state.'

Dated: Walla Walla, August 31, 1891.

Hugh McMillan

W. M. Clarke, Witnesses.

The Chinese consul-general in this city, will at once communicate these facts to his own government, and it is probable that steps will be taken to punish the murderers.

Lawrence Kansas Western Home Journal

October 1850

HORRIBLE MURDER.

We learn from Judge Wright, of Quindaro, that the body of a man was discovered a few days since, near the road about 4 miles this side of Quindaro. He had been shot through the body, and then his face literally chopped off and carried away so as to prevent recognition. His clothes also had been removed, except two shirts; the under one was of brown drilling with linen waistbands, the outer one of common red flannel. He was apparently a young man, of medium size, with curly black hair. No clue as yet been obtained of the perpetrators of this horrible deed.

AUTHOR'S COMMENTARY

The following two stories memorialized the criminal exploits of two teenage outlaws who happened to be girls. Jennie Metcalf and Annie McDoulet were indeed desperadoes, and their tender age captivated the nation.

The Butte Miner

Saturday, August 24, 1895

FEMALE BANDITS.

THE NEW WOMAN ASSERTS
HERSELF IN OKLAHOMA.

Perry, Okla., Aug. 23.

Jennie Metcalf (née Jennie Stephens) and Annie McDoulet the former 16 and the latter 14, are behind the federal prison bars on several charges. Both pleaded guilty this evening to selling whisky to Indians and stealing horses, and to-morrow officers will take them to the reform school.

These are two of the most notorious female outlaws that operated in this territory. Both are young and their career of lawlessness has been short, but they have made big reputations. Both ride astride, go heavily armed and wear big spurs. These women were arrested 50 miles east of here Sunday, but not till they gave the officers battle. Twenty shots were fired before they were captured, and both women were compelled to surrender, having run out of ammunition.

Jennie Metcalf, the elder of the girl outlaws, was arrested three months ago, dressed in men's clothing, for whisky selling. She was put down by officers as being very successful in whisky selling. She gave bonds after a few days in jail, and began selling at once and reveling in other crimes. A week ago she was arrested again and escaped, stealing her captor's only horse. Saturday evening the sheriff arrested her and she again escaped, this time while eating supper in a restaurant. She ran through the back door and tore off her dress as she ran, which left her in men's attire. Officers again arrested her Sunday night and succeeded in lodging her in jail.

Annie McDoulet has been a spy for a band of outlaws, and succeeded on many occasions in preventing their arrest. They go to a reform school tomorrow in preference to the penitentiary.

The Guthrie Daily Leader

Wednesday, November 4, 1896

SHE'S A GOOD GIRL NOW.

AUTHOR'S COMMENTARY

The story's title takes a great leap of faith. Did she move past her criminal ways or was the story written too early to know? From my experience in law enforcement, a high percentage of people become repeat offenders. Hopefully Jenni never reentered the criminal world since her story is too compelling to end in another prison sentence.

Jenni Metcalf, Once a Member of
Bill Doolin's Gang, Returns.

A few days ago a young lady passenger arrived in Perry and was driven to the Pacific hotel. In her healthful appearance, graceful bearing and pleasing countenance no one recognized the once female outlaw, Jenni Metcalf, known among the various bands of outlaws, with whom she formally associated, as "Little Breeches."

It is claimed she was led astray by Bill Doolin, and about six months afterwards married Robert Stephens, with whom she lived about six months. For several months she shared the vicissitudes and dangers of the remnant of the Dalton gang, and was afterwards with the Doolin and Cook bands.

She donned a complete male attire and carried a Winchester. Two years ago she was arrested and charged with selling whisky to the Osage and Creek Indians, to which charged she plead guilty, and on account of her age, being only 16 years old at the time, was sentenced by Judge Bierer in the District Court at Pawnee to two years in the Boston reformatory, Boston, Mass., where she remained one year, her father and relatives having secured a commutation of her sentence to that time.

A gentleman who lives in Perry, to whom she spoke freely of her former life and expressed deep regret for her waywardness, says she further stated she was completely reformed and, under the good treatment and discipline of the reformatory, had been led to denounce her former reckless life. She has returned to her father's home near Sinnett, in Pawnee county, where she intends to begin a new life.

AUTHOR'S COMMENTARY

The following stories speak for themselves. There is no commentary I could add to increase their understanding.

Fort Wayne Daily News
Thursday, November 8, 1906

MURDER VICTIM CHOPPED TO PIECES

BIRMINGHAM, Ala., Nov. 8.

Piece by piece the big county sewer is giving up the remains of an unknown man who, according to the verdict of the coroner's jury yesterday, "came to his death by violent means at the hands of persons unknown."

Eleven days ago the trunk of a body was found near the mouth of the sewer south of Bessemer. Later fragments of arms and legs were found. Tuesday a foot, encased in a new shoe, was fished from the sewer several miles from the sewer mouth. Yesterday a human skull was found in the sewer. The jaws were crushed in, evidencing foul play. Another leg and foot were also discovered yesterday. Wire and rope were tied to the leg and to the other end were attached pieces of rock. All efforts to identify the dead man or learn the manner and motive of his death have failed.

Arizona Weekly Citizen

Saturday, February 15, 1896

TELEGRAPHIC.

CINCINNATI, OHIO, Feb. 6.

Scott Jackson, accused of the murder of Pearl Bryan, of Green Castle, has confessed implicating Alonzo M. Walling. Walling has also confessed to a personal knowledge of the murder of the girl last Friday night. Walling tries to lay the whole blame on Jackson. A satchel which the murdered woman bought here January 28 was shown to Jackson to permit him to examine the bloodstains in it. He would not quite admit that the head had been in the satchel, but he said it looked as if it had been there. Will Wood, a son of Rev. D. A. Wood, of Green Castle, at South Bend, Ind., was also arrested on account of a telegram alleging that he might be an accomplice in the murder.

Later – Scott Jackson made a confession, by small statements, because he saw clouds of evidence gathering around him. He has not divulged the details of the crime. When he admits the girl was murdered he does it as if a third person had committed the crime. Jackson's roommate, Alonzo Walling, has confessed to knowledge of the crime, but only as a go-between Jackson. There is no doubt that Jackson was the principal. William Wood, arrested in South Bend Ind., is deeply implicated. A bundle of letters from Wood to Jackson bear this part of Jackson's confession out. Nearly all of Wood's letters are about girls and some too grossly indecent to be read aloud. Pearl Bryan would have become a mother in four months. Jackson says Wood is responsible for her condition.

Lancaster Intelligencer

Wednesday, January 5, 1881

A HORRID MURDER.

The Victim Chopped to Pieces.

SAN ANTONIO, Jan. 3.

A most atrocious murder was committed at a woodchoppers' camp, four miles east of this place, on Saturday night. Bruno Hilago, refusing to lend his sources to Juan Ray, who desired to go to San Rosa, Mexico, the latter felled him with an axe, and getting a shotgun, struck him over the head with the butt end of the gun. Then picking up the axe he literally chopped his victim to pieces and then fled, but has since been captured.

Buffalo Weekly Express

Thursday, December 30, 1897

USED A RAWHIDE.

OUTSIDER WENT TO AN ILLINOIS SCHOOLHOUSE AND FLOGGED TWO OF THE BOYS.

Galesburg, Ill., Dec. 29.

A sensational affair in the Cooke School, Orange township, has caused much excitement. A warrant has been issued for Nels Lindstrom. The story is that last Friday Lindstrom went to the schoolhouse while it was in session. He had a new rawhide whip. It is said that he was angry because of trouble which two of the pupils had had with his own children.

As his request, it is said, Mr. Anderson, the teacher, dismissed all the pupils save the two whom Lindstrom wanted. Lindstrom is accused of flogging the boys. According to the parents the children were covered with black and blue welts. The teacher, it is said, permitted the whippings.

AUTHOR'S COMMENTARY

Unfortunately, in today's society, we have all seen how often hideous criminals become celebrities due to the availability of twenty-four hour media coverage via the internet, television, and printed material. Charles Manson, Ted Bundy, Jeffrey Dahmer, and John Wayne Gacy have all become familiar names to most of us. It is shameful but, human nature being what it is, it will never leave us. The following story and editorial make it clear this was already a concern in the late 1800s. The more egregious and ruthless the criminal, the more media coverage the crime receives and, in turn, creates a legend of the criminal. For these reasons, I feel it's appropriate to end this book with the following story.

Boston Post

Saturday, July 18, 1891

SHOT THROUGH THE HEAD.

Miss Christie Warden Murdered
by a Rejected Lover.

HANOVER, N.H., *July 17.*

A shocking tragedy occurred here tonight. As Miss Christie Warden, accompanied by her mother, her sister Fannie and Louise Goodell, were returning on foot to their home, located one mile from the village, at a late hour, Frank Almy, about 30 years of age, jumped into the road in front of them, and seizing Christie by the arm said: "I want you." The mother and sister attempted her defense, when he fired at them but missed. They ran for assistance.

Then Almy dragged his victim into the bushes from the road and shot her twice through the head, one shot tearing out her left eye. When help arrived the girl was dead and her body was stripped of nearly every article of clothing. Almy had fled.

Miss Warden was a beautiful and most estimable young woman, about 25 years old a graduate of the State Normal School, and a popular teacher. Almy was a former employee of her father's whose attention Miss Christie repulsed. She was the daughter of Andrew A. Warden, a wealthy farmer and leading citizen. The terrible affair occurred so late that it was midnight before the news reached the village. Sheriff Foster is sending out searching parties in all directions, Almy is about 5'10" tall, has a dark mustache, and is of a pleasing address and is well educated.

The father of the murdered girl offers a reward of $500 for the capture of the murderer. The town will undoubtedly offer an additional reward.

News and Citizen

Thursday, August 27, 1891

From the Editorial Board

The tendency of humanity to make a hero out of a criminal is again forcibly shown by the attention given to the foul murderer, Almy. We fail to see where good can result from such attention, and while a criminal ought to receive fair and decent treatment, he should not be lionized and treated as if he were an honored guest and not a villain of the blackest character. The Boston Record speaks thus plainly upon the subject:

'Now we are having the silly season in regard to the murderer Almy. A more despicable murder never was committed, and yet to read some of the papers an ordinary

person would be likely to believe that, after all, the murder was only a demonstration of Almy's great affection for his victim. Yesterday the girl's father went to see Almy, and one of the papers says this morning that the latter "spoke very kindly" to the father of his victim. If we are not much mistaken, when all the facts are known, this Almy will turn out to be as hardened a villain as is often found, and the sooner he is put out of the way, and the less attention is given to making a martyr of him, the better it would be for all concerned.'

AUTHOR'S FINAL COMMENT

Grievously, crime has always been an inherent part of every society in the history of the world and the United States is no exception. Although we enact laws and punishments in efforts to reduce it, it is a part of living which we have no choice but to accept will always exist. Humans have many failings and inflicting suffering on another person is a tragic weakness found within far too many.

As you have read, much like modern times, there was no shortage of crime during the 1800s either. As long as human beings inhabit the earth, criminal activity will continue to exist.

PHOTOS

Belle Gunness and children

Black Woman Lynched

Bloody Benders

Charles Julius Guiteau, the assassin of President Garfield

Doc Holliday

Four Men Lynched

H.H. Holmes

Lt. Joseph Petrosino murdered by the Black Hand

Lynching

President Garfield

Ray Lamphere

Two dead members of the Dalton Gang. Bob Dalton second from left, Grant Dalton second from right

Wyatt Earp

*For More News About Mike Rothmiller,
Signup For Our Newsletter:*

http://wbp.bz/newsletter

Word-of-mouth is critical to an author's long-term success. If you appreciated this book please leave a review on the Amazon sales page:

http://wbp.bz/tcc1a

**AVAILABLE FROM ALICE KAY HILL
AND WILDBLUE PRESS!**

UNDER A FULL MOON by ALICE KAY HILL

http://wbp.bz/underafullmoona

AVAILABLE FROM ROD SADLER AND WILDBLUE PRESS!

KILLING WOMEN by ROD SADLER

http://wbp.bz/killingwomena

AVAILABLE FROM PATRICK GALLAGHER AND WILDBLUE PRESS!

'Til Death Do Us...' by Patrick Gallagher

http://wbp.bz/tildeathdousa

See even more at:
http://wbp.bz/tc

More True Crime You'll Love From WildBlue Press

A MURDER IN MY HOMETOWN by Rebecca Morris
Nearly 50 years after the murder of seventeen year old Dick Kitchel, Rebecca Morris returned to her hometown to write about how the murder changed a town, a school, and the lives of his friends.

wbp.bz/hometowna

BETRAYAL IN BLUE by Burl Barer & Frank C. Girardot Jr.
Adapted from Ken Eurell's shocking personal memoir, plus hundreds of hours of exclusive interviews with the major players, including former international drug lord, Adam Diaz, and Dori Eurell, revealing the truth behind what you won't see in the hit documentary THE SEVEN FIVE.

wbp.bz/biba

SIDETRACKED by Richard Cahill
A murder investigation is complicated by the entrance of the Reverend Al Sharpton who insists that a racist killer is responsible. Amid a growing media circus, investigators must overcome the outside forces that repeatedly sidetrack their best efforts.

wbp.bz/sidetrackeda

BETTER OFF DEAD by Michael Fleeman
A frustrated, unhappy wife. Her much younger, attentive lover. A husband who degrades and ignores her. The stage is set for a love-triangle murder that shatters family illusions and lays bare a quiet family community's secret world of sex, sin and swinging.

wbp.bz/boda

www.ingramcontent.com/pod-product-compliance
Lightning Source LLC
Chambersburg PA
CBHW050312120526
44592CB00014B/1882